Heartlander

AN AMERICAN JOURNEY

★ ★ ★

DICK HERMAN

with Victor Gold

EMERALD
BOOK CO.

To my wife Peg, who taught my family
and me love and respect for all.

This is a work of nonfiction, and the events are portrayed to the best of the author's memory.

Published by Emerald Book Company
Austin, TX
www.emeraldbookcompany.com

Distributed by Emerald Book Company

For ordering information or special discounts for bulk purchases, please contact Emerald Book Company at PO Box 91869, Austin, TX 78709, 512.891.6100.

Design and composition by Greenleaf Book Group LLC
Cover design by Greenleaf Book Group LLC
Interior photographs courtesy of the author.
Cover image: © Getty Images (US), Inc. (United States) / Fuse

Publisher's Cataloging-In-Publication Data

Herman, Dick, 1920-
    Heartlander : an American journey / by Dick Herman, with Victor Gold.—First edition.
    pages ; cm
    "Introduction by James A. Baker, III"—Table of contents.
    Issued also as an ebook.
    ISBN: 978-1-937110-67-3
    1. Herman, Dick, 1920- 2. Businesspeople—United States—Biography. 3. United States—Politics and government—20th century. 4. Autobiography. I. Gold, Victor, 1928- II. Baker, James Addison, 1930- III. Title.
HC102.5.H47 A3 2014
338.092/4   2014932963

Part of the Tree Neutral® program, which offsets the number of trees consumed in the production and printing of this book by taking proactive steps, such as planting trees in direct proportion to the number of trees used: www.treeneutral.com

TreeNeutral™

Printed in the United States of America on acid-free paper

14 15 16 17 18 19   10 9 8 7 6 5 4 3 2 1

First Edition

Other Edition(s):
eBook ISBN: 978-1-937110-68-0

Table of Contents

Introduction

BY JAMES A. BAKER III

If you were to end the tale of Dick Herman at his fortieth birthday, a little less than halfway through his life, it would be a tremendous success story, one that represents the eternal optimism, perseverance, and creativity that has made our country a great one. Born in 1920 and raised in small-town Fremont, Nebraska, his life started in the Roaring '20s and continued through the Great Depression, World War II, and America's postwar economic boom. Neither of his parents had a formal education. But this was a time in our nation's history when hard work and common sense paid dividends—even in rural Nebraska.

That, of course, was the American Dream, the dream that his parents—Mike and Dutch Herman—dearly believed in, strove to achieve, and taught their children, both in words and deeds. Mike Herman worked his tail off driving Nebraska's back roads to supply farmers with kerosene and gasoline. When he wasn't doing that, Mike was a regional salesman for Sinclair products. The jobs kept Mike away from home much of the time, but the rewards were gratifying. The Herman household was able to afford amenities that others couldn't—a refrigerator, an electric stove, and indoor plumbing. Meanwhile, Dick, the older of two Herman sons who shared a room their entire childhood, was earning his own spending money by selling newspapers on the street corner and doing other odd jobs.

By the time Dick was eight years old, the sun was shining favorably on the Herman family. But then, their household joined millions of others that were jolted on Black Friday in 1929, when the stock market crashed, starting a decade of financial hardship that gripped the United States and the world. A little more than a year later, the unthinkable happened. Dick returned home from school to find neighbors and friends in his front yard discussing a tragic car accident. At the age of thirty-five, Mike Herman was dead, the victim of faulty steering in his old truck.

Dutch and her two sons, Dick and Dale, faced a huge challenge. Cardboard soon filled holes in their shoes. A loud, off-handed comment by a fellow student that Dick was wearing someone else's hand-me-down coat stung sharply. But the three Hermans didn't flinch. Inspired by their mother's determination to keep the family business afloat, ten-year-old Dick began driving the fuel truck to serve their customers. Dale also picked up slack left in the wake of his father's death. Not only did the family business survive, but it also flourished, allowing Dick to go to the University of Nebraska and then enter the military during World War II, when he helped push the axis troops first out of North Africa and then Italy. After the war, Dick and his brother teamed up to build the family trucking company into a national giant. By the 1960s, each had diversified their own portfolios, entering other businesses that became just as prosperous.

For most people, the success that Dick Herman had gained by 1960 would be satisfying enough. But Dick was a part of what NBC news anchor Tom Brokaw has called "The Greatest Generation" in his book by the same name. Not only did those who lived through the Great Depression and World War II dedicate themselves to business and community volunteerism, as Brokaw points out, many of them focused on politics, seeing it as a peaceful way to enact change. And so, during the second half of Herman's life, the political chapters in his personal story are as interesting and rewarding as those in the first half.

That's where I came to know Dick Herman, through Republican politics. The two of us first met when I was delegate chairman for President Gerald Ford's 1976 primary campaign against Ronald Reagan. That was the last really closely contested primary election for president, and it wasn't decided until the Republican National Convention. After that, Dick and I worked together continually in subsequent presidential campaigns for Ronald Reagan and George H. W. Bush, and remained close friends.

What I have liked best about Dick has been his sharp, analytical mind, and particularly his keen ability to wade through difficult party decisions and develop winning strategies that can receive broad-gauged support. He believes strongly in the conservative principles that bind Republicans—limited government, lower tax rates, and less federal intervention. In 1964, Dick was a strong supporter of Barry Goldwater, who established his presidential campaign on the principle that "Extremism in the defense of liberty is no vice, and moderation in the pursuit of justice is no virtue." Dick traveled on the candidate's campaign plane and personally witnessed much of Goldwater's historic-but-losing campaign against President Lyndon B. Johnson.

Although he has been and remains a dedicated conservative, Dick also realizes that you have to win elections and then govern effectively if you want to transform political ideals into sound public policy. And so, sensible compromise is important to him. President Reagan was the same way, and he often said, "I'd rather get 80 percent of what I want than go over the cliff with my flag flying." That viewpoint always made sense to me, as well, and so it was rewarding for me to see Dick write about it as he recounts in his book the many political stories that he has witnessed firsthand—from Barry Goldwater to Richard Nixon to Gerald Ford to Ronald Reagan to George H. W. Bush.

Heartlander: An American Journey is an inspiring account of a life well-lived, of a Midwest gentleman who refused to see personal setbacks as anything but an opportunity to move forward and improve himself. But it is more. It is an insightful account of American politics as seen through the eyes of Dick Herman, a beautiful human being and a charter member of the Greatest Generation.

★   ★   ★

Whatever America hopes to bring to pass to the world must first come to pass in the heart of America.

— Dwight D. Eisenhower

Casablanca, Morocco

JANUARY 1943

Six months after entering the Army as a newly hatched ROTC lieutenant at Fort Warren, Wyoming, I found myself half a world away,
assigned to a desk fronting the entrance to the Anfa Hotel in midtown
Casablanca. My assignment: guardian at the gate, the first-line moni-
tor of all who sought to enter the site of the historic meeting between
President Franklin D. Roosevelt, Prime Minister Winston Churchill,
and the Free French leaders Charles de Gaulle and Henri Giraud.

This would be the conference that not only laid plans for the Allied
invasion of Europe, but also set out the terms for ending the war against
the Axis powers—Germany, Italy, and imperial Japan–nothing short of
an "unconditional surrender." It would also end with Roosevelt's naming
of an unexpected choice, General Dwight D. Eisenhower, as Supreme
Commander of the Allied Forces for the coming invasion.

All this was of course far above the pay grade of a 22-year-old junior
officer whose worldview before boarding a troop ship headed for North
Africa was limited to the rural stretch of eastern Nebraska that ran from
Fremont (population 8,000) to Omaha to the University of Nebraska
campus at Lincoln.

My job–whatever historic decisions were being made in Casablanca
that week–was to see that nobody got past the lobby of the Anfa Hotel
unless cleared by the command post upstairs. A simple enough assignment until one of the most recognizable figures of the North African

campaign walked through the doors–ramrod straight, cavalry boots gleaming, an ivory-handled pistol hanging from each hip. I rose and saluted. He returned the salute.

"I'm General Patton," he said. "I'm here to see General Marshall."

"Yes, sir." I picked up the phone and called Marshall's aide, Lieutenant Colonel Frank McCarthy, to announce Patton's arrival. Tell him, said McCarthy, that General Marshall's in a meeting and can't be interrupted.

Not surprising, since Marshall was Chairman of the Joint Chiefs of Staff and President Roosevelt's top military advisor. I hung up the phone and relayed the message to Patton.

"Thank you, Lieutenant," came the reply; after which, without breaking stride, he headed toward and up the staircase that led to Marshall's office. Orders or no orders, I just sat and watched. I may have been a country boy, but I knew enough to stand clear of George S. Patton when he had an objective in mind.

★   ★   ★

I

Mike's Dream

Let me tell you how you know that a barnyard cow is really ready to be milked: You first put one of the family cats to work a few feet away, aim the udder in his or her direction, then give a gentle tweak. If the stream is long enough for the cat to catch it on the fly, there's enough pressure to begin milking.

I learned that trick at a young age on my grandfather's farm in Nickerson, Nebraska, twelve gravel-road miles north of my family home in Fremont; at least it was a gravel road in the distant days when auto travel in the American heartland could be a bone-rattling adventure.

Still, visiting my grandfather's farm in the summertime was an adventure I wouldn't have missed, any more than I'd have passed up a chance to play pitch-and-catch with my father on days he wasn't working dawn to sunset delivering gas and kerosene to his farm customers.

Looking back, it was a boyhood of fond memories, but like the years it covered, from the Roaring '20s to the Great Depression, it had its highs and lows.

I remember the excitement that came with early radio, listening to the World Series between the St. Louis Cardinals and the Philadelphia Athletics, as well as the shock a few years later on learning that, as an *Omaha Bee-News* Extra told us, LINDBERGH BABY KIDNAPPED.

As a newsboy, I stood on a busy street corner in Fremont, shouting that headline until my supply of papers sold out. Over the years, it was only one of many jobs I worked at before and after school: delivering papers for the *Bee-News*; selling magazine subscriptions for *The Saturday Evening Post, Liberty*, and *The Ladies' Home Companion*; cleaning service station restrooms and summer camp latrines (I was known as Dan the lavatory man); oiling machines at the local power plant; soda-jerking at the Palace Cafe; and hardest, but most rewarding of all, helping my father unload gasoline tanks with a hand pump.

Nowadays they call that multitasking. Back then, we had a simpler word for it: necessity.

★   ★   ★

My father, Ralph—everyone called him Mike—was twenty-five when I was born August 6, 1920. My mother, Mabel—everyone called her Dutch—was twenty. I was their second child. Their first, Ralph Henry, died shortly after birth. My younger brother, Dale, was born in 1924, which meant a shared bedroom until I went off to college. Shared, but happy. Ours was a loving partnership, both in family life and business. It lasted a lifetime.

Like most young, rural Americans in those years, neither of our parents had much formal education. But what they lacked in schooling, they more than made up for in the willingness to work long hours and the native intelligence otherwise known as street smarts.

There was no G.I. Bill to help World War I veterans get a college education or a new start in life, but our father left the Army with his eyes set on something other than following in the footsteps of his own father.

A popular postwar song at the time was, "How Ya Gonna Keep 'Em Down on the Farm (After They've Seen Paree?)". Dad hadn't seen Paree—his service had been spent as an Army Air Corps mechanic in Texas. But he'd seen enough of the world outside Nickerson, Nebraska, to catch the commercial spirit of the times, going to work for Sinclair Oil after the war as the company's sole agent in Fremont.

It was a job that kept him working dawn to dusk, supplying farmers in the area with gas and kerosene for their vehicles and houses. Dad drove an old tank truck, filling it with fuel supplied by Sinclair via railroad. On top of that, he was called on to be a salesman for Sinclair products. But the job had its rewards, beginning with the wherewithal to buy an electric stove—no more cooking with burned corncobs and coals—and a General Electric refrigerator, replacing an old ice box (which, sad to say, meant no more free chipped ice from the horse-drawn ice cart). Not to forget, we were also one of the first families in the neighborhood to install indoor plumbing.

Things were looking up, enough so that in early 1929 Dad felt the time was ripe to expand his operations and begin a business of his own. He bought four acres of land adjoining the railroad tracks on the outskirts of town and signed a contract with Skelly Oil to be their wholesale distributor for the area. A small service station on the property served as his headquarters and two vintage tank trucks—one borrowed from my Uncle Merle Bruner—represented the sum total of his company inventory.

Brought up to believe that with faith and hard work all things were possible, Dad had a dream—to build a family business. He would call his new company Herman Oil.

★   ★   ★

Black Friday, October 29, 1929, the day the dreams of millions of Americans came crashing down: It was the beginning of a long decade of national hardship. But as the Christmas season of 1930 approached, what happened on Wall Street was far from the thoughts of an eight-year-old student at North Side grammar school in Fremont. A family visit to Brandeis & Sons department store in Omaha was in the offing. There would be Christmas lights, colorful decorations, crowds of holiday shoppers—all the excitement of the season my brother Dale and I could ask for.

It was a cold, crisp Nebraska day in early December. I was hurrying

home from school, looking forward to the trip when, turning the corner of North Union Street, I saw a crowd gathered in our front yard.
Neighbors and family friends, talking in hushed tones—a scene and
sound that stay with you, no matter how many years or decades pass: My
father was dead, killed in an accident only hours earlier while making
deliveries in our old country truck. A faulty steering wheel had failed
him as he approached a gravel road. He was only thirty-five years old.

★   ★   ★

America is still a country with thousands of rural towns, but today small
towns like Fremont, Nebraska, are linked to the outside world by the
wonder of mass communication. But in the 1920s and '30s, an age when
even radio and telephones were a novelty, the link that bound us together
was eye-to-eye, and neighbor-to-neighbor. And never so much as in a
time of tragedy.

On the morning of December 8, 1930, the Fremont Methodist
Church was filled to overflowing with mourners lined up in the street.
It was the largest funeral in town history, an outpouring of love and
affection for a friend and neighbor who, however brief his time on earth,
had left his mark on the community—a legacy for those who followed
in young "Mike" Herman's footsteps.

★   ★   ★

II

Dutch's Way

Dutch: My mother was given that nickname for good reason. She was physically small, even petite, but when Mable Williams Herman made up her mind about something, she couldn't be budged. She was strong-willed, plucky, and left the impression that had she been born half a century earlier, you would have found her handling the reins on one of those covered wagons headed west.

Mom was born two months before the turn of the century, October 28, 1899, in Mount Moriah, Missouri, of English (not Dutch) ancestry, moving to Fremont with her family at an early age. A sign of things to come was her single-minded ambition to play the piano, despite the fact that she couldn't read a note of music. Not only did she teach herself to play, but in time she became a first-rate pianist.

There was simply no quit in Dutch Herman. Like her husband, she was a perennial optimist who saw any and every obstacle in her way as a challenge to be overcome.

Never back off from a difficult job, Mom would say, just find a way to get it done. Not only did she preach that philosophy, she practiced it: To make ends meet she mastered the skill of keeping books for a local businessman as well as the art of hairdressing for her neighbors.

"Dutch" Herman wasn't about to give up her husband's dream, even in the worst of times. Herman Oil would not only survive as a business, it would grow in the way Mike had intended—Depression or no Depression.

★　　★　　★

With Dad gone, operating Herman Oil became a family enterprise in fact as well as name. Mom kept the books and handled the contracts, but with her feet barely able to reach the accelerator, I often became the designated driver in deliveries to our farm customers. While a ten-year-old driving a truck might raise questions today, it drew only passing notice back then, given the time and conditions.

Every family that lived through the Great Depression of the 1930s had its own painful memories. In the big cities jobless workers stood in soup lines while World War I veterans, denied the pensions they had been promised, sold apples on street corners, their stories summed up in an Al Jolson song, "Brother, Can You Spare a Dime?"

In farm communities like Fremont we saw families lose their life savings when banks closed down, while farmers were forced to kill and bury their hogs when the market for livestock hit bottom. I remember hungry drifters passing through town on rail boxcars, knocking on the back door and offering to work in exchange for food. Mom always gave them something to eat, no matter how hard it was to keep her own family fed and clothed from day-to-day.

There was always food on the table in the Herman household. I filled in as the cook-in-charge when it came to Swiss steak, chili, and cake-baking. Clothing was another matter. New shoes were hard to come by, and when the soles wore through on my old ones, I'd stuff them with cardboard until I learned how to resole and reheel them. Heels cost ten cents a pair, half-soles twenty cents, glue a nickel.

An incident involving not shoes but a coat comes to mind: I was walking by two schoolmates one day—girls whose names and faces I still remember—and one commented in a voice loud enough for me to hear, "Look, he's wearing Jack Slicker's old coat."

The memory stays with me after all these years for good reason. It was an embarrassment that led me to vow I'd never let it happen again. Not only a motivator in life, but also a reminder of how far we had to go to make Dad's dream a reality.

★   ★   ★

Her full name was Margaret Carolyn Martin, but everyone at Fremont High knew her as Peggy or Peg. She was the prettiest girl I'd ever seen and from the moment I first saw her I knew—and in fact told my best friend at the time, Ed Bremer—that I'd marry her someday. Call it vanity, call it clairvoyance, I just felt it in my bones. But there was a problem, beyond getting her to feel the same way.

It was no problem as far as I was concerned, but to my grandmother, Henrietta Williams, the idea of her grandson's even dating a girl of the Catholic faith was nothing short of heresy.

Religion and what she saw as God's will were at the center of Granny Williams' life. She was a true-believing member of the Free Methodist Church who got so carried away during Sunday sermons she would "see the Light" and fall into a dead faint amid a fundamentalist chorus of "Hallelujah" and "Amen."

It would take time for Granny Williams to see the light where her grandson and Peg Martin were concerned, but for that matter, it took time and distance to bring Peg and me together as a couple. We dated once as seniors at Fremont High, but it wasn't until we took separate paths after graduation that things got serious. She enrolled at Duchesne College, a Catholic all-girls school in Omaha, while I left for the University of Nebraska.

The year was 1937. I was seventeen years old, living away from home and family for the first time, and hard put trying to keep up with schoolwork while holding down jobs as a food-hasher at a sorority house and a night attendant at an off-campus filling station. But I'd saved up enough to buy a 1929 Model A Ford, the distance from Lincoln to Omaha was only fifty-nine miles, and by the end of our first year in college Peg and I were—to use an old-fashioned phrase—going steady.

*   *   *

Going to college was by no means a given for young Americans in the 1930s, but I was fortunate enough to have two aunts, Ethel and Laverle, who as schoolteachers preached the importance of a higher education. Add to that the fact that an uncle, Clairmont Herman, was a University of Nebraska alumnus, and it was clear that after graduating from Fremont High I'd be heading for the Nebraska campus at Lincoln.

It was, looking back on it, an eye-opening time for a small-town boy to be going to college. The summer before, in his acceptance speech at the 1936 Democratic National Convention in Philadelphia, President Roosevelt had coined the phrase "rendezvous with destiny" in speaking of the challenge facing young Americans: a high-flown phrase, but one that caught the spirit and mood of those prewar years.

Not yet out of the Great Depression, the country was slowly waking up to the threat posed by hostile dictatorships overseas. The full awakening was still years in the future, but looking ahead I joined the campus Reserve Officers Training Corps, ending up on the recommendation of my Phi Delta Theta fraternity brother, George Abel, in the ROTC, Quartermaster Division.

So it was, that only twenty years after my father's generation fought what they were told would be the War to End All Wars, I found myself drilling and learning military tactics as my generation geared up, slowly but surely, to answer the call to our rendezvous with destiny.

*   *   *

I was brought up in a family that didn't have the luxury of wasting time or taking detours. That said, my close friends at Nebraska, like George Abel and Cliff Meyers, were understandably puzzled when, at the end of my freshman year, I headed west to Seattle and transferred to the University of Washington. My Aunt Violet lived there and her husband, Freddy Boynton, was not only a successful lawyer but had strong contacts in the state's attorney's office in King County.

A law career beckoned—or so I thought at the time. The undergraduate courses I'd taken—political science, history, accounting, and statistics—fit into a pre-law pattern and I was drawn to the thought of being the first member of the Herman family to hang out a lawyer's shingle.

The thought didn't last long, however. Twelve months later I was back in Lincoln, on track to graduate with the Nebraska Class of '41, but there was Herman Oil to think of and my role in helping Mom build the family business. Not to mention the prediction I'd made back in high school: If I ever hoped to marry Peg Martin it was time to get back home.

★   ★   ★

January 1, 1941: Going into my final year in Lincoln, we rang out the old with a cross-country trip to Pasadena, to see our Nebraska Cornhuskers play Stanford in the Rose Bowl. Four of us—me, my roommate Cliff Meyers, Jack Bodell, and George Petrow—all packed into George's car.

The year gone by had seen Europe overrun by the Nazis and congressional passage of the country's first peacetime draft act. Ominous signs, but all put aside by four young Husker fans headed west. Passing through Reno, I hit the jackpot—seventy-five dollars!—on a slot machine. Pressing my luck, I bet a random Stanford fan twenty-five dollars on the outcome of the game. Honor system: The loser would leave the money at the other guy's hotel.

Final score: Stanford 21, Nebraska 13. I dropped the money off in a sealed envelope on our way out of town.

For the four of us—Cliff, Jack, George, and myself—it was a last
college lark. The following year, three weeks after Pearl Harbor, the
authorities considered the Rose Bowl crowds in Pasadena too tempt-
ing a target for the Japanese. The game was played in Durham, North
Carolina. And I was waiting for orders to report for duty.

★   ★   ★

III.

Getting It Done

Peg and I were married December 27, 1941, at St. Patrick's Catholic Church in Fremont. A joyous family gathering, but like most celebrations that took place that holiday season, it was clouded by thoughts of what lay ahead now that the country was at war.

The weeks and months after the attack on Pearl Harbor brought nothing but bad news from overseas. Not only had our fleet suffered crippling losses, but Japanese forces were overrunning American and British outposts throughout the Pacific and Southeast Asia. There were rumors of enemy submarines off the California coast, and fears heightened in the first week of June 1942 by news that Japanese troops had occupied the Aleutian islands of Attu and Kiska.

Fearful times—but if there's a single lesson to be learned from more than two centuries of American history, it's that nothing unites the American people more than an enemy attack on our native soil, whether it's Pearl Harbor or the Twin Towers.

Yet for those of us who've lived through both national tragedies, there's a big difference between the unity shown after the shock of December 7, 1941, and that following 9/11 sixty years later.

The country responded to Pearl Harbor with a total commitment not only in spirit, but in material sacrifice. As I packed my gear and prepared to report for duty in the summer of 1942, it was good to know that I was one of millions doing the same, while those on what was called "the home front" were doing their part on behalf of the war effort. There was food and gas rationing, along with bond drives and campaigns to recognize the sacrifice being made by those in uniform and their families.

That's anything but true today. At the time this is written, young Americans are fighting and dying in the Middle East after more than a decade of war following the attack on the Twin Towers and the Pentagon. But other than bumper-sticker support and hot-winded political speeches on patriotic holidays, you wouldn't know there's a war going on.

The powers that be in Washington call it "limited war." And that it is—limited and unfair to those Americans called on to risk and sacrifice their all, while on the home front, it's business (and pleasure) as usual.

I'll have more to say about this issue and what I, as a World War II veteran, see as the way to correct this unfairness in later chapters.

★   ★   ★

My orders came through on, of all auspicious dates, July 4, 1942: I was to report for active duty at Fort Warren, Wyoming, for six weeks of basic training. On the troop train headed west (with my college roommate, George Abel), I had no idea of what lay ahead or where I'd end up. What I did know, however, was that everything in life up to that point had taught me to expect the unexpected.

The word "proactive" wasn't around in those days, but it summed up my approach to handling whatever challenge I'd meet during my wartime years—beginning at Fort Warren.

It turned out I had an edge on other members of the training program because of my year spent at the University of Washington. While in Seattle I'd risen (with the help of a friend) to the rank of Cadet Captain of an ROTC unit. That would help during my years in service, but not until I'd learned to resist the impulse to take charge when I wasn't in charge—as happened during a marching drill not long after my arrival in camp.

What do you do when the man marching next to you is out of step? The rule is, take care of your own step and let the drill instructor handle the rest—which is why, after I'd shouted, "Let's get in step!" to the fellow marching next to me, the drill instructor called me down for talking in line and revoked my weekend pass.

Lesson learned, though grudgingly. I spent my weekend on base, but come Monday went to see the officer in charge of the program, Captain Ben Givens, to let him know that though the reprimand was proper, the punishment was excessive. A bad move, had I run into a short-tempered martinet. Givens, however, was a fair-minded officer who not only heard me out, but after I'd finished, to my surprise, appointed me head of the company!

Another lesson to pass on to recruits: If you're going to take on the way things are done in the military, make sure you've drawn the right officer. I'd pressed my luck one time and come out ahead. Going forward, I'd have occasion to press it again as I headed out of training camp for assignment overseas.

★   ★   ★

Now this is not the end. It is not even the beginning of the end. But it is, perhaps, the end of the beginning.

—Winston Churchill, reporting on the U.S.–British invasion of North Africa, November 1942

Operation Torch. It was the largest amphibian landing in history up to that time, three-hundred warships and four-hundred other vessels carrying more than 105,000 troops from the United States and Great Britain to nine landing sites in North Africa, some nine-hundred miles apart.[1]

It was also, as Winston Churchill said, the turning point of the Allied war effort against Nazi Germany, in the same way as the Battle of

Midway and the Marines landing at Guadalcanal had turned the tide of the war in the Pacific during the summer months of 1942.

Of the 105,000 troops landing in North Africa, 72,000 under the command of Lieutenant General Mark Clark embarked from ports in southern England; and 33,843, under the command of Lieutenant General George S. Patton, crossed the Atlantic in a ten-day convoy of crowded—in most cases, overcrowded—troop ships.

We were designated Task Force 34 (or Western Task Force) and though I can't recall the name of the ship I boarded that day eight decades ago, I still remember the sense of both excitement and relief that ran through our unit in finally learning where we were headed—a port named Casablanca in far-off Morocco.

For weeks the Ordnance Company I was assigned to at Camp Kilmer, New Jersey, had been waiting for orders to ship out, destination unknown. Peg, writing from Fremont, informed me that consulting with her all-knowing Ouija board she'd learned I'd soon be headed for England. It was as good a guess as any, given the shroud of secrecy the War Department had placed over the direction American involvement would take in the European theater.

General George C. Marshall, the Army chief of staff and President Roosevelt's top military advisor, had argued for a direct cross-channel invasion of the continent, England to northern France, in 1943, but the British general staff had other ideas: First, clear the Germans out of North Africa; then attack what Winston Churchill liked to call "the soft underbelly" of Nazi-held Europe; then conduct a cross-channel invasion of France in late 1943 or 1944. Marshall lost that argument. He later admitted it was just as well, as the North African and Mediterranean campaign not only weakened the Germans, but helped shape the American army into a first-class fighting force by the time the cross-channel invasion took place.

Crossing the gangplank that gray autumn day in 1942, I could look back on a hectic three-month period that had taken me from Fort Warren to Fort Lewis, Washington, then to Camp A. P. Hill, Virginia, and finally to Camp Kilmer, the point of embarkation. It would be more than three and a half years before I would again set foot on American soil.

In his history of the war in North Africa, *An Army at Dawn*, Rick Atkinson tells of the extensive preparations the Quartermaster Corps made in gearing up Patton's Western Task Force for the coming invasion. Each ship was crowded not only with men, but in Atkinson's words:

> Into the holds went tanks and cannons, rubber boats and outboard motors, ammunition and machine guns, magnifying glasses and stepladders, alarm clocks and bicycles . . . tractors, cement, asphalt, and more than a million gallons of gasoline, mostly in five-gallon tins . . . thousands of miles of wire, well-digging machinery, railroad cars, 750,000 bottles of insect repellent, and 7,000 tons of coal in burlap bags . . . black basketball shoes, 3,000 vehicles, loudspeakers, 16,000 feet of cotton rope, and $100,000 in gold coins, entrusted to George Patton personally. And into the holds went a platoon of carrier pigeons, six flyswatters and sixty rolls of flypaper for each 1,000 soldiers plus five pounds of rat poison per company. A special crate, requisitioned in a frantic message to the War Department, held a thousand Purple Hearts.

Still, for all those details, no master plan could take in all the possible glitches that could arise in a mass movement of men and materiel under wartime conditions. There were 10,000 men on board our crowded ship with nothing to do during daylight hours except gripe, as soldiers do, play cards, and wonder what the future held. A few minutes a day were set aside for calisthenics, but other than that no advance thought had been given to fundamental activities—such as lining up, thousands strong, to eat three times a day. The result was that some companies were overfed, while others—including my own—ended up on short rations.

It was time to speak up again, though I ran the risk that the colonel in command, one of General Patton's deputies, might not be as tolerant of complaints as my commanding officer back at Fort Warren. But once again I was in luck. Either the colonel was unaware of the problem or was so overwhelmed by other problems he was glad that someone, even a lowly second lieutenant, could come up with a solution.

"What's your answer, Lieutenant?" he asked after I'd laid out my complaint.

First, I said, we need to line up for chow only twice, not three times, a day; second, there ought to be an officer from every platoon checking off the men who've been fed so they don't go through the line twice before everybody's been through once.

Nothing brilliant about that. Just common sense. But as I learned—not only in the Army but in later life—common sense is often the first casualty when large numbers are involved in mass movements, military or civilian. (See, for example, later chapters on the planning and conduct of political conventions.)

All I'd come to ask for was equal chow rights for my company. I wasn't prepared for the colonel's response.

"Good thinking, Lieutenant," he said. "I'm putting you in charge of the mess hall."

So it was that though there was an officers' mess on the upper deck, I never saw it again. Making sure that ten thousand men got twenty thousand meals a day until we reached the shoreline in North Africa was a full-time job.

★   ★   ★

Mention Casablanca to a member of the Baby Boom generation of the 1940s and '50s and it brings up an image of wartime romance in an exotic North African city. I've seen the movie and liked it. But for those who landed there in November 1942—ground troops of George Patton's Task Force 34—our lasting memory is one of windblown sand, white stucco buildings on narrow, twisting streets, and more often than not, mass confusion.

We were an army just-arrived but on the move, our target destination being that "soft underbelly" of Hitler's Europe that Winston Churchill talked about.

The commanding general in charge of the invasion of southern

Europe would be Lieutenant General Mark Clark, not Patton, though Patton actually had more combat experience at the time. But in choosing Clark over Patton to head the Fifth Army that would invade Italy, General Eisenhower had in mind Clark's ability to work with the British and other foreign forces that would fill out the command.

Patton, as every American schoolboy knows, was anything but a diplomat. "Old Blood and Guts" was as direct and forceful in speech and manner as he was on the battlefield. I recall the first time I saw him, not long before he showed up at the front desk of the Anfa Hotel asking to see General Marshall.

It was late night on the Casablanca docks, where I'd been assigned to oversee the unloading and storage of equipment and Patton, ramrod straight in full combat regalia, came striding off one of the landing craft. Without saying a word he had the aura of leadership that would make him one of the greatest, if most controversial, military figures in American history.

Focused on the day-to-day duties of a junior officer assigned to ordnance logistics, I had little idea that Providence had put me in a place where not only the great generals but the great leaders of the world would meet for a historic conference that would shape the future of the war.

"It was there that Roosevelt announced that the Allies would accept nothing less than unconditional surrender from the Axis," writes Andrew Roberts of the Casablanca conference in *The Storm of War*. "It was also at Casablanca that Roosevelt and Churchill conferred on where to attack once the Germans were expelled from Africa. After much tough negotiation . . . Sicily was chosen the most direct route."

The invasion of Sicily (code-named "Husky") would be a joint American-British operation, with Patton in command of American troops, while Clark prepared the Fifth Army for the invasion of Italy (code-named "Avalanche").

My days under Patton's command were coming to an end, however. Not long after the Casablanca conference I was ordered, as one of one-hundred officers and enlisted men, to set up command headquarters for the Fifth Army. For the rest of the war I would serve under Clark as part of the Forward Echelon of Fifth Army Ordnance Headquarters.

★   ★   ★

I often thought what a tough old gut it was instead
of the soft belly he had led us to believe.

—Lieutenant General Mark Clark in a postwar comment on
Winston Churchill's belief that Hitler's Europe was like a crocodile,
with the Mediterranean its "soft underbelly."

Starting at the heel of the Italian boot—the landings at Anzio and Salerno—the Fifth Army met fierce German resistance on the way to Naples and Rome. Two of the bloodiest battles of the war were fought at Monte Cassino and at the Rapido River, where the Texas 36th Division suffered nearly three thousand casualties, more than half killed.

Some look back at the Italian campaign as a secondary diversion, a prelude to the D-Day invasion of France in 1944. But as military historians point out, along with putting Italy out of the war, Operation Avalanche and what followed tied up no fewer than nineteen crack German divisions.

As a member of the Forward Echelon, my job was to provide General Urban Niblo with intelligence on the movement of troops and supplies. That meant traveling in advance of our line, which often brought me into situations that pointed up the contrary nature of fighting in an enemy country where the people don't consider themselves enemies. In one village, our advance squad—a driver, an interpreter, and myself—were surrounded by friendly Italians shouting, "Viva America!" when we suddenly came under German shellfire. At that, our driver froze and I had to shove him aside, take over the wheel, and move our jeep triple-time to safety.

Though bitter fighting continued up the length of the peninsula—the

Germans were led by one of their best battle tacticians, Field Marshal Albert Kesselring—the climax of the Italian campaign would come with General Clark's triumphal entry into Rome, the first Axis capital to fall to the Allies. It was a dramatic moment in World War II history, but one quickly overshadowed by what took place the following day—the cross-channel invasion of France on June 6, 1944.

★   ★   ★

I had gained a reputation for sizing up problems and coming up with solutions by thinking beyond standard guidelines and following common sense instincts—the "Dutch" Herman formula for getting-it-done. In time it earned me promotions to first lieutenant, then to captain—my captain's bars pinned on by General Clark himself.

Early spring, 1945: With the war in Europe drawing down and after nearly three years overseas, I became eligible for a forty-five-day furlough. It was while sailing home that news came of President Roosevelt's death and the swearing-in of a new president, Harry Truman—a shock since FDR had been the only president most of us on board had known since coming of age. It was the first signal that the America we were going home to wasn't the same country we'd left when we shipped off to war.

★   ★   ★

The 1946 movie *The Best Years of Our Lives* won an Academy Award when it captured the spirit and drama of men returning home from World War II to family and friends, a moment in time shared by millions of American veterans. In my case, it began in Kansas City, Missouri, where Peg, "Dutch," and my brother, Dale, who had been serving in the South Pacific, met me at a crowded train station. In the days that followed I'd see and hold for the first time our daughter Mary Catherine, born when

I was still in North Africa, visit friends to share stories of what we'd experienced while I was away, and wait for orders on where to report when my leave was up.

My next overseas assignment, I'd heard, would be across the Pacific, possibly in China, to take part in the land, sea, and air campaign to finish off the last remaining Axis power, Japan. It would be, if the battles of Iwo Jima and Okinawa were any guide, a brutal, bloody campaign costing tens of thousands of lives on both sides. But President Truman's decision to bomb Hiroshima and Nagasaki in mid-August 1945 drove the Japanese to surrender on the battleship *Missouri* on September 2, and I was mustered out of the Army at the Rock Island Arsenal in Iowa a few months later.

Home again, to a changed America, with bigger changes yet to come.

★   ★   ★

IV.

The Transition Years

*The 1950s may be the most misunderstood decade
of the American 20th Century.*

—*The Fifties Chronicle*, Beth Bailey and David Farber

Underestimated might be a better word. Far from being the decade of national drift seen by some historians, the 1950s were years of far-reaching change in American life.

It was the U.S. Supreme Court's historic decision in the 1954 case of *Brown v. Board of Education of Topeka* and the Martin Luther King–led Montgomery, Alabama, bus boycott of 1955–1956 that sparked the civil-rights movement. On a lesser scale, the mid-'50s arrival of Elvis Presley and rock-and-roll forecast the youth revolution of the 1960s.

But the biggest impact on the nation's life in the '50s came in the twin fields of communication and transportation. Coast-to-coast television changed the way Americans looked at themselves and the world; Congress's passage of the Federal Highway Act of 1956 created a national network of interstate highways that brought the country together as never before.

As one history of the period put it, the federal highway system—officially known as the Dwight D. Eisenhower National System of

Interstate and Defense Highways—"contributed in shaping the United States into a world economic power."

In domestic terms, the national superhighway would come to replace the railroad track as the fundamental means of transporting people and products from city to city, state to state, coast to coast.

For an enterprise like Herman Oil Transport, this was literally the road to the future.

★   ★   ★

Dale and I returned from the war to find the family business had not simply survived, but thrived during our absence. Our fleet of trucks had expanded and Mom, with the help of business friends Abe Gendler and H. A. Reznick, had successfully moved our center of operations from Fremont to Omaha.

The oil transport business, once wholly dependent on the railroad industry, was in transition. Construction of the Omaha pipeline in 1940 had made it possible to bring petroleum products straight from the refinery to Omaha and Carter Lake, Iowa, just across the Missouri River. Mom was quick to realize that to remain competitive in the oil transport business we had to be situated as close to the pipeline as possible. Every out-of-line mile cut into operating costs.

So it was that the Herman family moved to Omaha, the new head-quarters for our expanding business. And expand we did, across state lines to all parts of the country. But not without our share of lean times.

Contrary to what's taught in most business schools, successful entrepreneurship isn't simply the result of having a sound business plan. You can lay out a brilliant plan, but as a general once said about going into battle, no plan survives real-time contact with the enemy.

The enemy, as far as running a successful enterprise is concerned, isn't so much your business competitor as unforeseen events. My friend Bob Devaney, who at one time was the winningest football coach in the country, once said that whatever success he had with his Nebraska team came not just by drawing X's and O's on a blackboard but from on-the-spot decisions he made in the flow of the game.

Knowing how to improvise—to respond to changed circumstances and move in a different direction—is the key to success in any enterprise at any time. It helped that my years in the military, as well as Dale's, sharpened our natural inclination to prepare for the unexpected, to deal with the day-to-day issues that faced a young, growing company in the volatile transportation industry of the postwar '50s and '60s.

★   ★   ★

Changing times call for changing ways. It's the first law of political or business survival. The politician who doesn't understand this gets swept out of office; the businessman who doesn't learn to adapt soon shutters his doors.

In every enterprise, there comes a moment when a decision has to be made that bends or otherwise alters your basic business model. By 1953, Dale and I, operating as Herman Brothers, Inc., found ourselves in a competitive bind brought on by our lack of reciprocity with a major oil company. Without reciprocity we were unable to purchase petroleum products other than the fuel we used to operate our own trucks.

The way out of this bind, obviously, was to make a deal with a trucking operation that had such reciprocity. To do that would require our offering up something that made a trade-off attractive to the other party. For more than three decades, beginning with Mike and Dutch, we had operated as a closed family operation. No outsiders, no partners. If the business was to survive, that would have to change.

Our partner would be a general commodities carrier, Interstate Motor Freight System of Grand Rapids, Michigan, owned by Larry Riley. A business friend, Hy Prucha, arranged a meeting with Riley to see if we could negotiate a deal.

My idea of negotiating is to save time and energy by getting directly to the point. In Riley's case I intended to make him an offer he'd find hard to refuse.

"Larry," I said no sooner than we were seated, "I'm here to offer you 25 percent of my company for a dollar if you'll give me control of your reciprocity."

Brief, direct, and effective: Herman Brothers Trucking would become partnered with Interstate Motor Freight; and later, extending our line of reciprocity further, with Standard Oil of Iowa (a tie-in that enabled us to take business away from our chief competitor at the time, Ruan Transportation).

Through the 1960s and into the '70s, Dale and I would see our business expand and diversify, partnering and working with major national operations like Northern Natural Gas, ConAgra, and Lone Star Cement. Our growing fleet of trucks would haul not only oil but flour, cement, propane, oxygen, and other volatile chemicals to and from terminals across the continent, from the Far West to Pennsylvania and New York.

Changing times, changing ways. And more often than not we stole a beat on our competition in making changes: Herman Brothers was the first major trucking company to go all-Mack, building the Thermadyne-driven tractor to our specifications to make it the best on the road. We were also among the first to bring time-in-motion expertise to the trucking business and to go before the Interstate Commerce Commission with an original rate-making system that the ICC not only approved but adapted for general use. And among the first, if not the very first, to work out an agreement with a major union that would change the way workers in the transportation industry, from truckers to airline employees, received their benefits.

★   ★   ★

The International Brotherhood of Teamsters is one of the oldest, most powerful trade unions in the country. It is also one of the toughest.

Driving monster-sized tractor-trailers long hours, day and night, what-ever the road or weather conditions, isn't an occupation that takes in the fainthearted or slack-muscled. Teamster leadership at all levels reflects that toughness. But if you're in the trucking business and hope to thrive, you learn to deal with it.

A story here about Herman Brothers most memorable experience in dealing with the Teamsters: We had built a terminal in Nashville to haul cement and it fell to Dale to travel to Tennessee and negotiate a contract with the union. When he arrived at Teamster headquarters, he was greeted by a burly union aide the size of a professional wrestler and escorted into a private office to await the arrival of the local's president. Then, with the muscleman standing directly behind him, Dale was pre-sented with the union's opening—and final—offer.

"He sat there," Dale reported, "opened a desk drawer, drew out a .38 automatic, and pointed it at me. 'Now,' he said, 'let's talk about negotiating.'"

End of bargaining talk. The only consolation was that we got the same contract terms as every other carrier operating in the area.

Fortunately, all our dealings with the Teamsters didn't run along those lines. There were times, in fact, that far from being adversaries, Herman Brothers and the union were partnered side by side to our mutual bene-fit, as occurred when the railroad lobby proposed that a Ton-Mile Tax be imposed on Nebraska's trucking industry. The year was 1956, and given the political clout of the railroad industry at the time, passage of the tax was considered likely.

But times were indeed changing. Railroads had dominated the country's political landscape for more than a century; but like the stagecoach, they were being supplanted by faster, more efficient means of transportation—motor vehicles over superhighways and airplanes that could cover in hours the distance it took railcars days to travel.

The Ton-Mile Tax was one of many desperate attempts by the rail-road industry to maintain its century-old monopoly over cargo trans-portation.[1] That it was defeated in a statewide referendum was due to the efforts of a broad-based coalition put together by Paul Halpine, head of the Nebraska Motor Carrier Association—a coalition that included truck operators, farm organizations . . . and the Teamsters.

Some would say the lesson to be drawn from that experience bears out the Sun Tzu proverb that the enemy of my enemy is my friend. But the fact is that—gun-wielding organizers aside—Dale and I never viewed the Teamsters as an enemy. As I told Frank Fitzsimmons, the Teamsters president I knew best, though Herman Brothers preferred operating nonunion for competitive reasons, we recognized the union's role in the industry and felt our mutual interests outweighed whatever differences we had.

Over time my relationship with Frank Fitzsimmons proved personally as well as professionally rewarding. We first met at a small dinner given by President Nixon on the occasion of the U.S.-Canadian conference on boundaries. The Teamsters, unlike the AFL-CIO, were not wedded to the Democratic Party (they still aren't), and a few years later, as vice-chairman of the 1972 Republican convention, I was asked by the President's re-election committee to invite Frank and his family to sit in my box. In later years, whenever Peg and I visited Washington, we would get together with Frank and his wife for dinner.

How, many people asked, could the competitive owner of a trucking company and the head of the Teamsters union break bread together as friends? It was a question framed by stereotypes that didn't take into account the common humanity we share with others. Despite the fact that Frank and I sat on opposite sides of the bargaining table, we shared the Depression-era experience of having worked our way up from humble beginnings in order to get to the table.

In his later years, Frank moved to La Costa, California. It was obvious his health was declining. It was during the Christmas season of 1980 that Peg took a call, with Frank at the other end of the line. He called, he said, to wish us a happy holiday season, and more. "I'm in the hospital," he told us. "I'm dying and just wanted to let you know I love you both."

Frank died a few months later. Memories of that call and his friendship have stayed with me.

✳   ✳   ✳

Not that change and growth during these transition years was confined to the business world. In the early 1950s, when Catherine was still a pre-teen, Peg and I made a decision to grow our family through adoption. Going into our middle years we could count among our blessings a full house—two girls, two boys—to fill out our lives: Cathy, Anne, Rick and Mike.

Both Rick and Mike would in time take part in the family business, a new generation to carry on my father's dream; though by the 1970s the business itself was moving in a direction my father could never have imagined.

✳   ✳   ✳

The successful business entrepreneur doesn't wait for opportunity to knock, he goes looking for it. My interest in a possible beer distributorship began in the late 1960s, a time when Joe Coors and I struck up a friendship.

It was also a time when the Coors beer label, a popular regional brand, took off on the national market as the elite brew preferred by malt connoisseurs like actor Paul Newman. The actor, a liberal Democrat, would later part with Coors, switching to Budweiser, as a protest against Joe's conservative Republican politics.

Republican politics, of course, along with a passion for what was then the Big Eight conference, was a common bond Joe and I shared. Peg and I would join Joe and his wife, Holly, at annual Nebraska-Colorado games, where the conversation would range from what was taking place on the football field to what was going on in the political world.

Diversifying with the beer business was a possibility my brother Dale and I had discussed many times, our sights set on operating the first Coors dealership in Nebraska. Operating a beer distributorship—provided you had the right product—required less maintenance and brought on less daily stress than running an interstate trucking company. But though my eye was set on Coors, once again the ongoing principle of the Herman family—expecting the unexpected—would come into play.

My lawyer at the time, Jimmy Ryan, was anything but a nine-to-five worker. Twelve noon, twelve midnight, it was all the same to Jimmy when he had news of a pending opportunity. His opening remarks that particular night in early 1970, via a late-night phone call, went like this:

> *I know you want Coors, and I don't know if and when*
> *a Coors distributorship will ever be available in Nebraska.*
> *But I do have a client in Lincoln who has an Anheuser-Busch*
> *distributorship that's available right now. My personal*
> *opinion, I think Budweiser is better than Coors.*

Better, that is, as a business venture. Not that there was anything wrong with Coors, but Budweiser was, as advertised, the "king of beers" as far as sales volume was concerned. A product of the Anheuser-Busch brewing company out of St. Louis, "Bud" became nationally famous as the prize-winning beer at the Philadelphia Centennial Exposition of 1876. It was—and remains—Anheuser-Busch's premier label, dominating a fiercely competitive market of U.S. and foreign beers, not only because of imaginative sales promotion but technical innovation: A-B, for example, was the first brewer to use refrigerated railcars for the shipment of beer.

There was a downside to our taking over Budweiser's Lincoln dealership, however. For the first time, Dale and I would be physically separated in our business operations. Somebody had to be in Lincoln to run the show—somebody competent, somebody we could trust—and when my first choice, a former Republican state chairman, begged off for personal reasons ("My mother is a Methodist and I can't be involved with alcohol"), the job fell to Dale.

The year was 1970. At the time, closing the deal for Budweiser's Lincoln operation seemed only another way to diversify, opening the door to a new venture, as D&D Distributors. Opportunity was waiting and we'd come calling. It didn't take long, however, to learn that this particular door was different from all those we'd opened in the past. It would lead us not only into a new field but a new vista.

★   ★   ★

Our friends are retiring and you're starting out on a new venture.

That was Peg's initial reaction to news that we were on the verge of taking over one of Anheuser-Busch's Los Angeles distributorships.

She was right, as usual. By 1981, I was well into my middle years and by all material measure a candidate for retirement. The Herman family trucking business had flourished, Mother having lived to see her husband's dream come true ("Dutch" would die August 9, 1991). Our holdings were such that Dale and I were able to go our separate ways in business, my taking over the trucking company while he became sole owner of the Lincoln distributorship (Dale would pass away on September 10, 2002).

I was in a position to leave the hustle and bustle of competitive business behind me. Retirement, however, is easier for some than for others. I enjoy playing golf as much as anyone, but I enjoy it more when I don't have the feeling there's an office I ought to get back to. And in 1981 I still had that feeling.

The Los Angeles Anheuser-Busch operation was quite a step up from the one we'd been operating in Lincoln in 1970 and the one we'd acquired in Grand Island, Nebraska, two years later. Those were profitable ventures, but only a fraction the size of A-B's beer business in southern California, a widespread territory that stretched from Malibu to San Pedro, with more than three thousand accounts.

It was one of Anheuser-Busch's biggest, but the company's St. Louis headquarters had little doubt it was in the right hands, especially

after looking over the board roster I'd assembled, which included leading political figures from both parties, including former Democratic
National Committee Chairman Bob Strauss.

Where Peg was right, the thing I'd overlooked, was the fact that it
wouldn't be possible to manage this king-sized business operation from
an Omaha base; or for that matter, to manage both a major trucking
operation and a major beer distributorship with the same level of energy
and attention to detail I put into a workday.

Something had to give. Hard as it was to part ways with the business I'd been in all my life, when Earl Wood, executive vice president of
Herman Brothers Trucking, proposed to buy the company, I took him up
on his offer, knowing the business would pass into capable hands.

Peg and I had lived our entire lives in Nebraska, but if I was going to
run a Los Angeles beer distributorship, it was clear we'd have to move
west. So it was that for the next decade and a half we would be resident
Californians. But wherever we lived, our hearts remained in Nebraska.

★   ★   ★

I thought we were friends.

—August A. Busch III to the author, circa 1985

It wasn't as if Peg and I were strangers to the California scene. Over
the years we'd visited there many times and made friends through contacts at Republican National Conventions. Settling in, I even got into
California politics in a limited way by actively supporting GOP guber-
natorial candidates.

I never fooled myself, however, into thinking I knew as much about
California politics as I did about Nebraska's. Every state has its own
political chemistry and the Golden State's, as history tells us, is more
volatile than most. In the fifteen years I spent there, a radical shift in
the balance of political power took place due to the growing influx of
migrant workers across the Mexican border.

In 1986, Congress, recognizing immigration from Latin America was a national issue, tried to deal with it through Simpson-Mazzoli, formally called the Immigration Reform and Control Act; a bill that, as it turned out, neither reformed nor controlled the problem of dealing with a rapidly expanding population of Hispanic immigrants.

Eight years later, California, through a voter initiative, moved to handle the issue on its own. Proposition 187 went on the ballot in 1994 with the aim of establishing "a state-run citizenship screening system to prohibit illegal aliens from using health care, public education, and other social services." It passed by a wide margin but after being challenged in the federal courts was set aside five years later as unconstitutional. Its political fallout, however, lingers to this day.

California, as 20th-century history tells us, was once a strong Republican state, producing two presidents in Richard Nixon and Ronald Reagan, and nationally prominent leaders such as Earl Warren, Tom Kuchel, Bill Knowland, and Bob Finch. For the past two decades, however, California Republicans have been so weak that only one member of the party, Arnold Schwarzenegger, has been elected governor, and then only because of name recognition in a free-for-all campaign after a Democratic governor was recalled.

What happened? Obviously, a backlash. When California Republicans took the lead in pushing through Proposition 187 in 1994, the state's growing Hispanic population reacted by turning against the party. Where the Hispanic vote had once been divided, it now swings solidly Democratic.

What's more, the reaction didn't stop there. Within a matter of months after the 1994 vote, we saw Budweiser sales go down in Mexican-American areas while the sale of a rival beer, Corona, brewed in Mexico by Cerveceria Modelo, were climbing. Politics aside, our Latino customer base was sending a message. In short order Bay Distributors, the operating name of our Anheuser-Busch franchise, was supplementing its Budweiser sales with those of Corona.

A second message wasn't long in coming, then, one not from California but St. Louis. My conversations with August A. Busch III up to that point had been cordial, but I could tell by the edge in his opening words that this was anything but a cordial call.

"I thought we were friends," said the president/CEO of Anheuser-Busch.

"We are friends," I replied. "What makes you think otherwise?"

My marketing Corona, he said. Even if it was only a fraction of our volume of Budweiser sales, I shouldn't be handling a competing product.

I explained the marketing situation in southern California, the special appeal a Mexican-brewed product had for Hispanic customers, but my explanation fell on deaf ears. Busch was in St. Louis, half a continent away. It was like trying to describe a combat situation in wartime to a commanding general fifty miles behind the lines.

The marketing men at Anheuser-Busch finally came to see things my way—that all the promotional and advertising dollars in the world weren't going to bring Mexican-American customers back to Budweiser. In 1993, Anheuser-Busch purchased 50 percent of Cerveceria Modelo, and Anheuser-Busch in southern California began marketing Corona along with Budweiser.

As of that 1985 phone call from St. Louis, however, it was clear that the Hermans' days in Los Angeles were limited. As I said at the time, a businessman should never fall in love with an asset. In February 1996, Bay Distributors was sold to Anheuser-Busch, and became a company branch. Offered a cash settlement, I opted for Anheuser-Busch stock.

No hard feelings. Los Angeles or Omaha, "Bud" is still my favorite beer.

★   ★   ★

V.

In Your Heart:
The Goldwater Campaigns
(1960–1964)

I'm going to lose this thing and I'm going to lose it big,
but I'm going to lose it my own damned way.

—Barry Goldwater to Bob Mardian, October 1964

"Dick calls politics an avocation," Peg once wrote, "but it's more than that. It's a major career, a commitment."

Right again. As a partner-in-life for more than half a century, Peg came to know me better than I know myself. Much as I thought of it as an avocation, politics drew me into what became a second career. Specifically, Republican politics.

It may come as a surprise to those I worked with (as well as against) over the years, but when I first went to register, at age twenty-one, I was undecided whether to sign up with the GOP or the Democrats. Dale and I had been working with a law firm in Iowa run by a member of the Democratic National Committee, an elder with a persuasive argument as to why any up-and-coming young man ought to join the party of Jefferson, Jackson, and Franklin Roosevelt. The Republican Party, after all, had been out of power in Washington for a decade and its prospects for the future looked bleak.

Not that I saw myself entering the political arena as a candidate. But given FDR's popularity at the time—he had just been elected to a third term—the case for registering as a Democrat wasn't without merit. One of the prime principles in understanding politics—or for that matter, any competitive endeavor—is that everyone wants to be with a winner.

But there was another factor in play, one that no member of the Herman family could ignore: My grandfather David had been a Republican stalwart back in Nickerson, Nebraska, and for a heartlander the matter of family tradition trumps any thought about winning or losing.

★　　　★　　　★

In a way, my ambivalence about party affiliation at a young age reflected the ambivalent nature of Nebraska politics in general. The Cornhusker State isn't easy to pigeonhole when it comes to party labels.

Looked at from the Eastern Seaboard, Nebraska is often seen as a stronghold of right-wing conservatism. Yet this is the state that produced William Jennings Bryan, the populist scourge of Wall Street at the turn of the 20th century, along with George Norris, the maverick Republican senator who championed labor's right to strike and who earned a chapter in John F. Kennedy's *Profiles in Courage* for his antiwar stand in the years leading up to World War I.

And more: Nebraska is the state that sent conservatives like Carl Curtis, Kenneth Wherry, and Roman Hruska to the U.S. Senate in the 1950s, then followed up in the 1980s and '90s with Bob Kerrey, a liberal Democrat, and Chuck Hagel, a moderate Republican later appointed Secretary of Defense in a Democratic administration. Though seen from the Eastern Seaboard as the heartland of conventionality, it's the only state in the Union to use the unconventional model of a unicameral, nonpartisan legislature.

It was while working with the legislature in the state Capitol at Lincoln that I got my grounding in politics, under the tutelage of Paul Halpine, head of the Nebraska Motor Carrier Association.[1] Going up against high-powered railroad lobbyists on issues like the Ton-Mile Tax, I learned that getting things done in the political arena is a matter of seeing all sides of a problem, not just your own talking points. Paul was the master of politics as the art of the possible. He recognized and taught me that compromise is the oil that lubricates the machinery of a democratic society.

★   ★   ★

Bill Spear, one of the keenest political minds in Washington at the time, became my second political mentor. Bill, who'd served as Nebraska's Republican state chairman, later moved to Washington to head Standard Oil's legislative office in the Nation's Capital. Eight years my elder, he was the experienced hand who introduced me to the national political scene.

July 1960. I'd had my first exposure to a Republican national convention in 1956, when another Standard lobbyist, Charlie Barr, got me posted as a C.Q. officer—Charge of Quarters, an upgrade title for someone who answers phones and delivers messages—at the Chicago convention that renominated President Eisenhower and Vice President Nixon.[2] Four years later, working alongside Steve Shadegg, Barry Goldwater's chief campaign strategist, Peg and I would find ourselves caught up in one of the most dramatic moments of the convention that nominated Nixon for president and Henry Cabot Lodge for vice president.

As head of the Republican Senatorial Campaign Committee, Goldwater had sent Shadegg to Nebraska to help in the re-election campaign of Senator Carl Curtis. Thanks to Bill Spear's recommendation, I'd been named Curtis' Douglas County (Omaha) campaign chairman. It was a challenge—carrying the urban areas of the state was the key to Curtis winning the election—but one that gave me an opportunity to test ideas I had on how grassroots political campaigns should be run.

Shadegg and I hit it off from the very beginning. I respected his experience and expertise as a political campaign consultant and he respected my knowledge of the area and the organizational skills I'd learned in the Army and the business world.

At that point, political campaigns in Nebraska were still being run the way they'd been run in my grandfather's day, when candidates reached voters by knocking on doors and handing out leaflets. Working with Shadegg, I laid out a plan to extend our candidate's reach by use of grassroots organization, the telephone, and professional polling.

By today's digital-world standards, all that seems fundamental. Tens of millions of dollars are laid out in congressional campaigns for grassroots outreach, telecommunications links, and focus groups. But in 1960 the Curtis campaign's use of mass mailings, telephone banks, and expert polling was considered revolutionary. Curtis was re-elected by a wide margin, and Shadegg, impressed with the effort I'd put in, asked me to lend a hand in future campaigns, using the same organizational model.

So it was that on a hot summer's day in Chicago, Steve, Peg, and I were in an office not far from the 1960 convention site, putting together a nomination speech to be made by Arizona Governor Paul Fannin—a speech that the nominee, Barry Goldwater, had agreed to only on condition that he'd then make a follow-up speech rejecting the nomination.

It was vintage Barry, the reluctant candidate, setting a pattern his supporters would come to know in the months and years ahead.

★   ★   ★

With the death of Ohio Senator Bob Taft in 1953, the conservative wing of the Republican Party found a new champion in Goldwater, an outspoken junior senator from Arizona who said he'd come to Washington "not to pass laws but to repeal them, not to initiate new programs but to cancel old ones, not to expand government but to extend freedom."

Words that captured the spirit of Republicanism, as understood by heartland conservatives. But there was no chance Barry Goldwater could capture the Republican nomination in 1960.

After eight years as vice president, Dick Nixon went into the convention that year as the party's all-but-certain presidential nominee. The only serious opposition to a Nixon nomination had been from New York Governor Nelson Rockefeller, the favorite of the liberal Eastern wing of the party. This was the same East Coast establishment that had controlled the party machinery for a quarter century, offering voters only what Taft and now Goldwater called "a me-too copycat" response to the liberal policies put forward by Democratic administrations.

Nixon, though admired for his anti-Communist record as a member of Congress, remained a question mark to many conservatives. In trying to bridge the gap between the two wings of the party, the Vice President left himself open to the charge of being a political opportunist. When news surfaced that he'd traveled to New York before the convention to discuss the platform with Rockefeller, it added fuel to the argument that for all his professions of conservatism, Dick Nixon wasn't to be trusted.

Rockefeller's campaign had put pressure on Nixon from the party's liberal wing. Fannin's nomination of Goldwater would balance the scales. It was a warning that conservatives were not to be taken for granted.

So there we were, in a small office on South Michigan Boulevard, Shadegg and I writing and Peg typing Paul Fannin's nomination speech, in what would be a prelude to one of the most memorable moments of the 1960 convention—not Fannin's lead-in, but Barry Goldwater's response to it. Lee Edwards, in *Goldwater: The Man Who Made a Revolution*, described the convention scene:

> Fannin took the podium as planned and called on Republicans to pick Goldwater "as the voice of conscience speaking for the conservatives of the nation." This man, said Fannin, "enjoys the love and affectionate regard of millions of Republicans who have never seen him. This man has challenged the imagination of America."

Then came the moment, as Goldwater went to the podium and, after a tumultuous ovation, delivered what some said at the time was his finest speech. After releasing his pledged delegates and suggesting they give their votes to Nixon, Barry talked directly to the true believers who had pushed his nomination.

"We are conservatives," he said. "This great Republican Party is our historical house. This is our home. Now some of us don't agree with every statement in the official platform of our party, but I might remind you that this is always true in every platform of an American political party.

"We can be absolutely sure of one thing: In spite of the individual points of difference, this Republican platform deserves the support of every American over the blueprint for socialism presented by the Democrats."

Now came the words that led another Arizonan, liberal Democratic Congressman Morris Udall, to call it "the beginning of the nation's conservative upsurge":

"This country, and its majesty, is too great for any man, be he conservative or liberal, to stay home and not work just because he doesn't agree. Let's grow up, Conservatives. We want to take this party back, and I think some day we can. Let's go to work."

Written by Jay Hall, the speech was a harbinger of better convention days to come for Republican conservatives. Four years later, the revolution Barry Goldwater promised came to pass.

★   ★   ★

It all started with a draft movement—a *genuine* draft movement, because the candidate, for all his dedication to the conservative cause, had no burning ambition to become president.

A week after the draft movement was announced in April 1963, Barry Goldwater made it clear that although he wanted conservatives to "take the party back," he had nothing to do with any effort to make him the Republican presidential nominee in 1964.

"I don't want the nomination," Barry told *The New York Times*. "I'm not looking for it. I haven't authorized anybody to look for it for me."

Had he stopped there, leaders of the draft movement—Clif White, Bill Rusher, and Peter O'Donnell—might have had second thoughts about trying to push a stubborn Barry Goldwater into a race he didn't want to run. But Barry being Barry, he let his innermost thoughts be known to the *Times* reporter: "But who can tell what will happen a year from now?" he asked. "A man would be a damn fool to predict with finality what he would do in this unpredictable world."

The door was obviously open, wide enough for a seasoned political operator like Clif White to take the Draft Goldwater movement to the next level.

Through Steve Shadegg, I became active in the campaign to make Barry the Republican Party's presidential nominee in 1964, my enthusiasm heightened by time spent with the Senator at a dinner party at Steve's house in Phoenix (I furnished the Omaha steaks, Peg cooked the onion rings).

No doubt about it, there was an appeal about Goldwater—even his opponents had to concede it—that no conservative leader before him could claim. As Theodore White put it in *The Making of the President 1964*:

> Tall, six foot even; a muscular 182-185 pounds; not lithe, with dancing steps, as was John F. Kennedy, but slow and dignified of walk; the face a deep tan, as is common among people who live in the sunlands; the frame of the face all sharp planes—the nose clean and sharp, the jaw pinpointed with one vertical dimple, the lips thin, the cheeks flat, no hint of the sagging jowl that normally overtakes men of his age, fifty-five. All this topped off by the silvery white hair set off by the black horn-rimmed glasses that made him instantly recognizable.

Then, White continued, there was the compelling way in which Goldwater presented the conservative case:

> The dry voice of the Southwest, far lower pitched than the Eastern voices that have dominated American politics for so long. It drawls in private questioning but becomes a snap when offended. . . . He is at his best in formal public address where, with the audience booming applause, his voice rises to a rhythmic roar (Goldwater has a good ear for the cadence of English prose) and develops the pounding wrath of an Isaiah. And altogether, all qualities combine to give a sense of hard virility and barely controlled tension.

Finally, heartland Republicans had a leader who could deliver the conservative message in a way that appealed to the grassroots voter. But any idea that a party takeover would occur without a fight was quickly dispelled. A "spontaneous" write-in campaign for Henry Cabot Lodge in the New Hampshire presidential primary signaled that the Eastern establishment was hell-bent on blocking a Goldwater nomination.

Lodge, we knew, was only a straw candidate. The real opposition would come from Nelson Rockefeller, and in case he faltered, Pennsylvania Governor Bill Scranton. The fight for delegates would go all the way to the California primary, where Barry pulled out a victory due in part to Rockefeller's having left his wife of many years to marry a younger woman.

Typically, though the fight for the nomination was one of the most bitter in decades, Barry pulled back from any mention of Rockefeller's private life in his campaign. As Lee Edwards wrote in his Goldwater biography:

> Most conservatives saw the controversy over Rockefeller's marriage as a heaven-sent disaster for the Republican Party's number-one liberal, but Goldwater was uncomfortable with the shift of emphasis from public issues and politics to personalities and private lives.

Goldwater, we were to learn, saw himself as a spokesperson for, rather than a leader of, the conservative movement. He viewed his mission as spreading the message, a teacher rather than a political messiah.

Mike Bernstein, chief Republican counsel on the Senate Labor Committee for both Bob Taft and Goldwater, was fond of telling a story to illustrate this view of the Arizona senator. It involved a conflict in Barry's itinerary because his staff had scheduled him to speak before two groups on the same day. The first was a conference of the National Association of Manufacturers, the second a student assembly at a Midwestern college.

As Bernstein recalled, everyone assumed the Senator would appear before the manufacturers, a source of funding for his campaign, and send a substitute speaker to the college. Instead Barry sent Bernstein to the manufacturers' conference, preferring to go before the students himself, spreading the conservative gospel to the next generation. It was politically impractical, but as Bernstein said, "If you worked for Goldwater you grew accustomed to the fact that he didn't do things the usual political way."

If he were ever to run for president, Barry confided to friends, he'd offer voters a clear-cut choice between the liberal vision of big, centralized government and the conservative vision of limited government and individual freedom. He even talked to President Kennedy—they were personal friends despite their political differences—about the two of them touring the country in a series of Lincoln-Douglas type debates, arguing domestic and foreign politic issues, liberal versus conservative, coast to coast.

Kennedy's assassination in November 1963 put an end to that idea and, as far as Goldwater was concerned, any realistic scenario for his winning the presidency. As Barry told his press secretary, Tony Smith, "There's no way people are going to vote in favor of having three different presidents in two years."

The Senator wasn't alone in that belief. As columnist Bill Buckley wrote after the election, "The Archangel Gabriel running on the Republican ticket could not have won" in 1964.

★　　★　　★

"No candidate ever came to a national convention better organized than the Goldwater for President Committee," wrote one observer in the press gallery at San Francisco's Cow Palace in July 1964.

With Nebraska's own Carl Curtis as floor leader, we were split up into six regional divisions. Clif White later recalled, "The (six) regional directors were the key to the whole convention operation."

Lloyd Waring directed Region One, which took in New England plus New York; Ed Failor was in charge of Region Two, the Middle Atlantic states, plus Kentucky and the District of Columbia; Wayne Hood had Region Three, the Great Lakes states; John Grenier had Region Four, the Southern states; I had Region Five, the Midwestern states plus Oklahoma, North and South Dakota, and Colorado; with Steve Shadegg handling California and the Far West.

As Peg commented at the time, my role at the Cow Palace that year was a considerable upgrade from what it had been eight years before, answering phones and running messages.

With the Rockefeller campaign out of gas, Bill Scranton had moved up as the great liberal hope for the presidential nomination. As the Goldwater delegate count grew day by day, the Pennsylvania governor, who had no real appetite for a fight with Barry (the two had been friends in past years), nevertheless found himself being used by liberal dead-enders, including a senior member of his staff, William Keisling.

In a vitriolic letter written by Keisling over Scranton's name, Goldwater was accused of leading a "radical extremist" movement that stood for a "crazy-quilt collection of absurd and dangerous positions"—a fairly extreme charge coming from a so-called "moderate" member of the party. And the Scranton letter didn't stop there. Goldwater's delegates, wrote Keisling, were nothing more than a "flock of chickens whose necks will be wrung at will."

The letter was hand-delivered to the Senator at Goldwater's Mark Hopkins Hotel suite on the eve of the convention. It was a pointless gesture in terms of doing anything more than rousing Barry's fighting instincts. That, according to some, might have been its real purpose—to get Goldwater angry enough to say something inflammatory that would turn off delegates who were on the fence. Instead, following a suggestion made by his campaign manager, Denny Kitchel, Barry sounded a conciliatory note publicly while following another suggestion, made by Ed McCabe, the campaign's research director, that copies of Scranton's letter be sent to every delegate.

The result was predictable. As a convention floor director charged with getting the "wrung chicken neck" letter into the hands of Region Five delegates, I had a firsthand look at its impact. We were fairly confident of winning the nomination going into the convention, but, as Clif White predicted, the Scranton letter would guarantee we'd go over the top on the first ballot.

It also guaranteed, as columnist Bob Novak reported, that any idea Barry might have had of naming Bill Scranton his running mate would be scrapped. His choice for running mate: upstate New York Congressman Bill Miller, whose great virtue, as Barry put it, was "he drives the Democrats nuts."

★   ★   ★

Extremism in the defense of liberty is no vice, and
moderation in the pursuit of justice is no virtue.

It would set the tone for the whole Goldwater presidential campaign— nineteen words that told the world this was no traditional party nominee. The lines weren't written by Barry's usual speechwriter, Karl Hess, but by Harry Jaffa, a professor of history who was only paraphrasing, he said, what Tom Paine had written in *Rights of Man*.

Reaction to the line was immediate. Whenever a presidential candidate is nominated after a hard-fought campaign, whether Republican or Democrat, the expectation is that he'll move to the middle. Jaffa's nineteen words, delivered by the candidate with emphasis, put that notion to rest.

There would be no moving to the middle or tacking to the political winds for Barry Goldwater. It would be a presidential campaign like no presidential campaign before or after. But it would be Barry's campaign, and nobody else's.

★   ★   ★

As Midwest Coordinator of the Goldwater campaign (appointed by National Chairman Dick Kleindienst), my job was to oversee operations in Nebraska, Oklahoma, Missouri, Kansas, Texas, North Dakota, and South Dakota.

That didn't mean my input to the campaign was limited to those states. Along with other Goldwater supporters close to campaign operations, I could see that for all the enthusiasm of Barry's crowds, our candidate was headed for a landslide loss. By mid-October the polls showed us thirty to forty points behind.

Even with that lead, however, the Johnson White House showed no sign of letting up on the Democrats' all-out attack on the Senator as an extremist intent on having a nuclear showdown with the Russians.

Nothing fixed the image of Barry Goldwater as a nuclear warmonger in the public mind more than the TV commercial the Johnson campaign ran on the CBS network in early September. Known as "the Daisy Ad," it showed a small girl pealing petals from a daisy, then an atomic bomb exploding, followed by the message, "Vote for President Johnson on November 3. The stakes are too high."

The ad ran only one time, but that was enough. With Nikita Khrushchev blustering in Moscow during one of the most dangerous periods of the Cold War, it frightened voters into believing that a ballot for Goldwater would mean total war with the Soviet Union and the end of civilization as we know it.

Piling on, there was also the Democratic National Committee's depiction of Goldwater as a racist, a charge based on his vote against the Civil Rights Act of 1964. This charge personally wounded Barry more than any other. He took pride in his lifetime record of having worked for racial equality as a storeowner, a city official, and a military reservist in Arizona. Having voted in favor of the Civil Rights bills of 1957 and 1958, he made it clear that his opposition to the 1964 bill was based solely on his belief that two sections of the '64 bill were unconstitutional.

Ignored by the DNC was the fact that two senior Democratic senators, Albert Gore of Tennessee and William Fulbright of Arkansas, had voted against the bill on the same grounds, Gore being the father of the future vice president and Fulbright being a political mentor to his fellow Arkansan, young Bill Clinton.

Summed up, as one writer later put it, "To the voters of 1964, Barry Goldwater seemed a lonely, some said loony, voice ordering progress to stop." It was a view that Barry himself, in his inimitable way, took at campaign's end when he told a reporter, "If all I knew about Barry Goldwater was what I read in the papers and heard on television, I'd have voted against the son-of-a-bitch myself."

★   ★   ★

For true believers, hope breathes eternal, even when the polls show your candidate is dead in the political water. The problem, we all believed, wasn't just the White House distorting Barry's record and the liberal press piling on, but our candidate's playing into their hands in his speeches.

Was it really necessary to talk about changing the Social Security law in a speech to an audience of retirees in north Florida? To criticize farm subsidies in North Dakota? To tell a crowd in Knoxville, Tennessee, headquarters for the Tennessee Valley Authority, that if elected he intended to sell off TVA and get the government out of the power business?

Along with other campaign directors, including Bob Mardian, I felt that much as we loved the Senator's straight talk, if he wanted to win the election he'd have to cool the rhetoric.

It was Bob who was given the unhappy task of delivering that message while aboard the Goldwater campaign plane. Somehow, rumor mills being what they are in political campaigns, word had reached Barry of our unhappiness with the way things were going. Bob's thought was that once the plane took off he'd ask for an audience with the candidate and make his pitch. As it turned out, he didn't have to wait that long to get his one-on-one meeting, though it didn't go the way he intended. No more than five steps into the plane's cabin, Bob was stopped by the candidate and told to sit down beside him:

"Mardian," said Goldwater, "I know what you're up to, but I want you to get one thing straight. I'm going to lose this thing and I'm going to lose it big, but I'm going to lose it my own damned way."

★   ★   ★

The bumper stickers showed up no more than two days after the votes were counted. They read 27 MILLION AMERICANS CAN'T BE WRONG. Lyndon Johnson had his landslide. But doing things his "own damned way," Barry Goldwater had managed to get more votes than any losing presidential candidate in history. He would go down—though he hated the description, calling it "sacrilegious"—as the John the Baptist of the conservative movement.

It was late in the campaign that someone suggested that Ronald Reagan, who headed California Citizens for Goldwater-Miller, should televise a speech he'd been making on behalf of the ticket—an appeal to voters titled, "A Time to Choose." Though it wasn't enough to turn the tide in Barry's favor, Reagan's appearance on national television was called, even by critics in the national press, the best speech anyone had made in the campaign.

Two years later, with "The Speech" as his launching pad, Ronald Reagan was elected governor of California. The party takeover Barry had promised was underway.

★   ★   ★

AS I REMEMBER
by Stu Spencer

The Republican primary battle that took place in California in 1964 between Barry Goldwater and Nelson Rockefeller is the first time my path really crossed with Dick Herman's, or shall we say, that I paid attention to him. My firm Spencer-Roberts was running the campaign for Rocky and Dick was deeply involved in the national Goldwater effort. Our campaign had one major problem that had to be addressed, which would be best termed "Family Values": Rocky's recent divorce and quick remarriage and the timing of a new child by his second wife.

Our basic strategy was, first, to define Goldwater as impulsive, not to be trusted in the nuclear age, and, second, to clean up Rocky's past meanderings. Addressing the second point, Rocky's schedule was loaded with appearances at church-oriented institutions—fundamentalists, black churches, and mainline religious groups, especially Catholics. Rocky's campaign had scheduled a major speech to be held at Loyola University, a Jesuit school, and at the time the most prominent Catholic university in southern California.

One Monday morning we woke up and were informed by the university that Rocky's speech had been canceled. We discovered that a man from Omaha was moving around southern California trying to undo Rocky's appearance at Loyola. This person turned out to be Dick Herman, a converted Catholic—and you know what they say, converts are the worst kind. His approach was poisoning the well with the whole hierarchy of the Los Angeles Archdiocese, including Loyola's vice president, other professors, and, of course, the large Catholic donors to the university. Also, Cardinal Thomas Francis Aloysius McIntyre himself had received a call from his fellow bishop in Omaha. What a coincidence.

Did it help the Goldwater campaign? Look at the following facts: 1) To be dumped from a major university as a scheduled speaker was not good press and raised too many questions; 2) In January 1964 Rocky was trailing Goldwater in California 58–27; but 3) In June 1964 Goldwater defeated Rocky in California by only 1 percentage point. Repeat, by only 1 percentage point.

I have always been hesitant to say that any one factor can affect the outcome of a political contest. But as I look back on 1964 I'd have to say that Dick Herman made a significant impact on political history.

VI.

The Nixon Years (1)
1968–1971

*The big winner in 1966 was Richard Nixon, who now saw his path
to the nomination in 1968 open up. Widely written off as a political
has-been after his loss to Pat Brown in 1962, Nixon had supported
Goldwater two years later when so many other Republicans stayed
home or supported Lyndon Johnson . . . . The political credits he gained
would turn into delegate votes two years later.*

—from *Grand Old Party: A History of the Republicans*,
by Lewis L. Gould

Bill Clinton was fond of calling himself The Comeback Kid, but his
ability to rebound from political defeat paled in comparison with Dick
Nixon's.

If Nixon's narrow loss to John F. Kennedy in 1960 wasn't enough
to end his political career, his loss to Pat Brown in the 1962 California
governor's race should have been, especially after a post-election news
conference in which he all but wrote off his political future. Republicans
still remembered his bitter words after that defeat—"You won't have
Nixon to kick around anymore, because, gentlemen, this is my last press

conference"—when the former vice president arrived at the national
convention in San Francisco two years later. Some even wondered why
he'd bothered to show up. With two losses behind him, events seemed to
have passed the former vice president by.

But Dick Nixon had something going for him that outside observers
couldn't see. He didn't move crowds with his oratory, but at small gatherings he could awe political insiders with his mastery of facts and figures.
Few if any public figures in his time could match Nixon's grasp of both
the big picture and the small details of issues, especially in the area of
foreign affairs.

What's more, though he was depicted by the press as cold and
self-involved, Nixon could call up not only the names of those he met
at gatherings but the names of their spouses and children. It was a personal touch that drew people to him—even those skeptical about the
true nature of his political beliefs.

It was during the Goldwater campaign of 1964 that Nixon laid the
groundwork for his political comeback. He came to the '64 convention
as a declared "neutral" in the fight between Goldwater and his liberal
opponents, Nelson Rockefeller and Bill Scranton; though press corps
cynics speculated that what the former vice president really wanted was a
Goldwater-liberal deadlock, with the convention turning to old reliable
Dick as a compromise candidate. However true that might have been, it
was what Nixon did after the convention that brought conservatives to
his side when the race for the 1968 presidential nomination came down
to the wire at Miami.

While Rockefeller and Michigan Governor George Romney sat on
their hands in the fall of 1964, Nixon had traveled coast to coast on behalf
of the Republican ticket, top to bottom. The effort paid dividends in terms
of conservative support. Added to that, the former Vice President's tireless
campaigning on behalf of Republican candidates in 1966 was fresh in the
memory of delegates arriving at the 1968 convention in Miami.

★   ★   ★

For the third convention in a row, Nelson Rockefeller was putting his time and personal fortune into a campaign for the Republican presidential nomination. And for the third convention in a row, the New York governor would come up short.

George Romney had made a run earlier in the campaign, but dropped out after trying to switch his position on the Vietnam War—from supporting to opposing it—by explaining he'd been "brainwashed" by the generals in the field.

Rockefeller came to the '68 convention in Miami after having alienated a large number of delegates during the primary process. Eight years before he had entered the race for the nomination, then dropped out, then re-entered it, leaving the impression he was indecisive. The experience obviously taught him nothing: He did the same thing in 1968, this time not simply disappointing but angering many supporters.

Maryland Governor Spiro Agnew, an early Rockefeller supporter, had gone so far as to invite reporters into his office to watch what he thought would be his candidate's announcement that he was running. When Rockefeller instead announced he wasn't running, Agnew was humiliated. The wheels were in motion that would make the Maryland governor not just a Nixon supporter, but a prime contender for the vice presidential slot on the national ticket.

Enter John Mitchell, Nixon's law partner in the New York firm of Mudge, Rose, Guthrie & Alexander. The former Vice President had named Mitchell his national campaign director, despite the fact that Mitchell had no prior campaign experience. What he did have, however, were wide political contacts due to his expertise in the municipal bond field; not to mention, a steel-trap mind and the cool, unflustered judgment that Dick Nixon looked for in a top-level advisor.

Mitchell knew Agnew not only from his contacts with the Maryland governor but from Agnew's days as chief executive of Baltimore County. When it came time for Nixon to pick a running mate, Mitchell's counsel would carry a great deal of weight.

But before that point was reached, there was the problem of Nixon's actually winning the presidential nomination. It was no sure thing, though he had the best campaign organization working the convention floor.

Along with Wayne Hood of Wisconsin, I'd been asked by Mitchell to oversee key state delegations. Wayne would work the north-central states and I was responsible for the Midwest. The campaign slogan was "Nixon's the One," a line meant to project the notion that his nomination was inevitable. The message was: *Get on board, the train's leaving the station and you don't want to be left behind.*

What those of us inside the Nixon campaign operation knew, however, was that while our delegate support was wide, it wasn't deep. Unlike Goldwater four years earlier, Dick Nixon's appeal wasn't one of ideological passion but political practicality: The argument was that if Republicans wanted to recapture the White House, Nixon was our best bet. He might not be everything conservatives wanted, but who else did we have? Certainly not Nelson Rockefeller.

The problem was that a late-entry alternative had shown up in Miami: Ronald Reagan, the conservative hero of '64 and now governor of California, claimed he wasn't a candidate for president, but a well-organized convention team was working full-time on his behalf.

Along with Goldwater campaign veterans Wayne Hood, Bob Mardian, and Fred LaRue, I liked Reagan but didn't see him as a ripened presidential candidate. His two years as California's governor gave him national appeal but Republican tradition told us that in any two-way fight for a presidential nomination, the nod went to the candidate who's paid his dues. On that score, Dick Nixon was far and away the One.

Still, as Mitchell and those of us working the convention floor knew, when a charismatic candidate appears on the scene, tradition can be swept aside. Conservatives learned that hard lesson in 1952, when Eisenhower defeated Taft. If Nixon didn't carry the day on the first ballot, we were in deep trouble.

Wayne Hood and I worked into the early morning hours the day the presidential nomination took place to hold our north-central and

Midwestern delegates in line, reporting our progress to Mitchell. The real threat, however, came not in our areas but in the South, where Reagan's appeal was on a par with Goldwater's in 1964. This was Fred LaRue's territory, but holding the line in states like South Carolina and Florida would take the efforts of someone more influential than Fred. Someone like Strom Thurmond, South Carolina's senior senator.

Thurmond's argument against anyone defecting to Reagan was brief and straightforward: Ron was a fine young man and someday might be a fine presidential candidate, but Nixon's national experience gave us our best chance of winning. The Democrats were divided and the White House was within our grasp. Why take a chance on a candidate who's never been tested nationally?

With that, South Carolina, Florida, and the rest of the Southern delegations held for Nixon and we won our first-ballot victory—but only by the narrowest margin in Republican convention history.

What was it about Dick Nixon that made every presidential vote he was involved in a nail-biter?

★　　★　　★

Alone among reporters covering the 1968 Republican convention in Miami, the *Washington Post*'s David Broder predicted Spiro Agnew would be Dick Nixon's choice as his vice presidential running mate. Broder's logic was that Nixon would see Agnew, the Republican governor of a Democratic state, as a running mate who would appeal to a broad cross-section of the party rank-and-file.

That wasn't the way critics of Nixon's choice saw it, however. Agnew's being on the ticket, according to these media pundits, was part of a "Southern strategy," a racist appeal to voters in the old Confederate states. The charge was leveled despite the fact that Agnew had won the Maryland governorship running against a racist Democratic opponent.

It struck me at the time—and still does—that while Republican candidates campaigning for Southern votes are portrayed in a sinister light, no such shadow fell over the Democrats when they dominated Southern politics under segregationist rule for nearly a century.

Did anybody accuse Franklin Roosevelt or John F. Kennedy of pursuing a "Southern strategy" when they ran for president while catering to the segregationist bias of what was then called "the Solid South"—meaning 100 percent Democratic? Were Roosevelt or Kennedy accused of racism when they stood by while members of their own party filibustered against civil rights legislation in the Senate?

I have always seen racism as a national rather than a regional problem, an issue that shouldn't be subject to partisan debate. But when charges are made that Republicans are pursuing a racist strategy, I feel called on to point out that without the votes of Republicans, led by Illinois' Everett Dirksen in the Senate and Ohio's Bill McCulloch in the House, Lyndon Johnson would never have been able to enact the Civil Rights Acts of 1964 and the Voting Rights Act of 1965. Those were the laws that broke down the walls of segregation and put an end to the racist political and social discrimination African-Americans knew during the years the Democratic Party pursued its own "Southern strategy."

★　　★　　★

BRING US TOGETHER

*—Sign greeting Republican presidential candidate
Richard Nixon on a campaign stop, October 1968*

With the exception of Roosevelt vs. Hoover in 1932, no presidential campaign in the 20th century was waged in more turbulent times than the race between Dick Nixon and Hubert Humphrey in 1968. Actually, it was a three-way race because third-party candidate George Wallace, though he had no chance of winning, would have a marked impact on the way the campaign was conducted.

Leading up to the fall campaign, the year had been one of bloodshed and violence. The country was torn by two assassinations, Martin Luther King Jr.'s and Bobby Kennedy's, along with race riots and anti-Vietnam War demonstrations in cities and on college campuses. The Democratic Party was in turmoil, with President Johnson having stepped out of the race for re-election and Hubert Humphrey having won the presidential nomination after a chaotic convention in Chicago.

All this seemed to point to a landslide win for Nixon-Agnew. With the Democratic left threatening to sit on its hands because of the Vietnam War and George Wallace's third-party candidacy carrying the South, Humphrey's prospects looked bleak. But then, as one observer put it, Nixon got overconfident and began campaigning cautiously, as if "not to lose."

Operating in the field as Midwest coordinator, I could see the race tightening as the Democratic base came together after Humphrey broke with the Johnson White House, coming out against the Vietnam War. By the last week in October, Humphrey had closed the gap to eight points and was picking up strength daily.

On Election Day, Peg and I joined John Mitchell and other campaign coordinators and strategists at the Waldorf Astoria hotel in New York. We came in hopes of celebrating the first Republican presidential victory in a dozen years, but as the night wore on it became apparent that the Nixon jinx was holding up: This election would be another nail-biter.

At 3:00 a.m., with the race still neck and neck, Peg and I excused ourselves and went to our room. Ninety minutes later I got a call from Larry Higby, a campaign strategist, asking if I'd check on a problem that had come up in my territory: For some reason, poll officials in certain areas of Missouri had stopped counting votes.

What was up? I put in a call to our Republican state chairman in St. Louis and he proceeded to give me a postgraduate course in campaigns and elections.

"There's no problem," he said. "We just heard they'd stopped counting votes in Cook County, Illinois, so knowing how that works . . ."

In short, there would be no political déjà vu all over again. In 1960, after a delayed vote count in Chicago Mayor Dick Daley's Cook County, John F. Kennedy had narrowly carried the state, and the election. What my friend on the other end of the line in St. Louis was telling me—and the world—was that the Nixon team this year wasn't taking chances.

"Tell Mitchell not to worry," said the St. Louis chairman. "We're just waiting for the Illinois results before we resume counting." Then the political punch line: "Nixon will win Missouri by 20,000 votes." (A statement I let stand, not really wanting to find out how he knew.)

I hung up the phone and reported the Missouri returns to John Mitchell. It was good news, followed by even better news a few hours later when Hubert Humphrey conceded defeat.

The long wait was over. As I headed toward the press area where a crowd had gathered for our candidate's appearance, I felt a tap on the shoulder. It was the president-elect, Mitchell at his side: "Herman," he said, "you were right about the Missouri count."

That I was, thanks to my clairvoyant friend in St. Louis. How he could tell the exact margin of Nixon's victory in Missouri hours before the final vote count remained a mystery. Whatever the answer, Dick Nixon had finally won a close one. And won it, as it turned out, with payback to Dick Daley and the Cook County political machine. In the final vote count, even Illinois went to Nixon-Agnew.

★   ★   ★

We take it for granted, but one of the most remarkable things about our system of government is the peaceful transition of power. It's the American process: No matter how heated the campaign or close the outcome, once the votes are counted and certified we turn the page, the verdict accepted.

In 1960, there were those who advised Dick Nixon to challenge the outcome of his election loss to John F. Kennedy based on charges of vote fraud in Cook County. Nixon rejected the advice because, he said, it would tear the country apart.

Forty years later, Al Gore took the vote count in Florida to court, but finally conceded the election to George W. Bush, asking his supporters to set aside their personal feelings and accept the outcome, for the good of the nation.

Like all losing presidential candidates, Hubert Humphrey was bitterly disappointed by the outcome of his race against Dick Nixon in 1968. But being Hubert Humphrey, the bitterness didn't run deep. His Democratic supporters called him the "Happy Warrior," a man with strong political convictions tempered by a warm, outgoing personality. Whatever Humphrey thought of Nixon's politics, he bore him no ill will. The country was the important thing.[1]

Unfortunately, the same couldn't be said of those Humphrey supporters who were congenital Nixon haters. From his earliest days in politics, running for the House against Jerry Voorhis and for the Senate against Helen Gahagan Douglas, Dick Nixon was marked as a man these Democrats loved to hate. His comeback and election as President in 1968 was attributed by this faction as a result of his—in the words of one such critic—"playing on the worst fears and darkest instincts of the American people."

Fortunately, this view of the results of the 1968 election wasn't shared by the Johnson White House, unhappy as Lyndon Johnson was about his Vice President's defeat. The transition from a Democratic to a Republican administration in 1968 would go as smoothly as the transition from a Republican to a Democratic administration had gone eight years before, when Kennedy replaced Eisenhower and Johnson had moved into the Vice President's office, replacing Dick Nixon.

It was the peaceful transition of power we expect from our leaders—the glory of our system and for more than two centuries, the envy of the world.

★   ★   ★

A few days after I returned to Omaha, I got a call from John Mitchell, asking me to be a member of the Nixon transition team. With John in charge, the team would be tasked with selecting and vetting nominees for the presidential Cabinet and sub-Cabinet, along with appointments to key agencies in the new administration. Along with Bob Mardian, I was sent to Washington to set up transition headquarters.

It's been said that one way to tell if an incoming president is sure of his ability to lead is by gauging the strength of those he picked to head up his administration. History tells us that strong leaders aren't afraid of being overshadowed by members of their Cabinet, the best example being Abraham Lincoln and his Team of Rivals.

President Nixon, as we look back at him four decades later, was a man ridden by insecurities, always on guard against those he considered political enemies. But none of that figured in the choices he made to fill out his Cabinet, beginning with John Mitchell, the Attorney General labeled by biographer James Rosen as "the Strong Man."

Nor was Mitchell the only heavyweight in the Nixon Cabinet, with names like William Rogers (State), Mel Laird (Defense), David Kennedy (Treasury), George Shultz (Labor), Bob Finch (Health Education and Welfare), George Romney (Housing and Urban Development), and Cliff Hardin (Agriculture), filling out the roster.

Cliff Hardin had been Chancellor of the University of Nebraska. As a member of the university's board of regents, I knew him to be not just a great administrator, but one of the country's leading scholars in the agricultural sciences. I also knew that in his laser-like focus to get the job done, Cliff, though a lifelong Republican, would take an apolitical approach to the job of administering the massive bureaucracy that made up the Department of Agriculture.

Sure enough, Cliff's confrontation with the White House Personnel Office wasn't long in coming. When asked to replace one of USDA's Assistant Secretaries, a Democrat, with a Republican, Cliff refused on grounds that the Democratic incumbent was extremely competent and didn't deserve to be fired. There would be no showdown. Unhappy as the White House was, Cliff, in his own quiet way, let it be known that as

Secretary of Agriculture, he'd run USDA in the way he thought best for the country, not the party.

Personnel matters aside, the White House had to be pleased with what Cliff was able to achieve in the three years he spent as Secretary of Agriculture. In addition to getting Congress to cut back on subsidies to the biggest farms, he not only extended the food-stamp program but established the Food and Nutrition Service for the poor.

Along with Cliff's joining the Cabinet there were three other high-level appointments I took a personal interest in during the transition: Dick Kleindienst, the Arizona friend I'd worked with during the Goldwater campaigns, was named Assistant Attorney General under Mitchell; Bob Mardian became Bob Finch's General Counsel at Health, Education, and Welfare; and John Warner, another member of the transition team, moved in as Assistant Secretary of the Navy. (Three years later, with the resignation of John Chafee as Secretary, John would take over the job and become a member of the Nixon Cabinet.)

Questions came up about my own interest in playing an active role in the new administration. My answer was no; I had a business to run back in Omaha. Though the Nation's Capital is a great place to visit, living in Washington had little appeal for either Peg or me.

Six months later John Mitchell would call me aside at a fundraising dinner held in Nebraska for Senator Roman Hruska to say that he and the President had a job in mind that wouldn't require a move to the capital. With my interstate trucking background, John said, I was the perfect candidate to take over as United States Boundary Commissioner, a quasi-diplomatic assignment that would require only my working with my counterpart on the other side of the Canadian border.

But that was down the road. First there was the matter of wrapping up the transition and joining our friends in celebrating the inauguration of the original Comeback Kid, Richard Nixon.

★   ★   ★

The White House, January 21, 1969

It was a long way from Fremont, Nebraska, in more ways than one. But there we were, Peg and I, at the Champagne breakfast the Nixons hosted for their supporters. To be in the White House itself was reward enough for the work put in to help elect the 37th president, but the Champagne was an added touch.

Every president in my lifetime has started out with high hopes and expectations, including Franklin D. Roosevelt at the lowest point in the Great Depression. The hope of most Americans in January 1969 was that Dick Nixon would bring the country together as he'd promised during the campaign.

That was the hope, but the expectation was something else. The Vietnam War and racial tensions following the assassinations of Martin Luther King and Bobby Kennedy had divided the country into hostile camps. Not a spring, summer, or fall had passed in the final years of the Johnson administration without a march on Washington and demonstrations in major cities that often led to violent confrontations between the police and young protesters.

Running for President, Nixon had said he had a "secret plan" for ending the war in Vietnam. Whatever it was, it would be put to the test in the months and years ahead, along with whatever hope he had of bringing the country together in difficult times.

All this had to be going through the new President's mind as he mixed and mingled with the crowd celebrating his inauguration in the East Wing of the White House that cold day in January 1969. After eight years in the political wilderness, Dick Nixon was back in Washington, his comeback complete.

For my part, after three months in Washington as a member of the transition team, I was ready to return to family, friends, and business. A White House waiter passed, carrying a tray of Champagne flutes. I shook my head, no thanks; at which point Peg nudged me and whispered,

"Dick, I really want to tell our friends back home we had Champagne at the White House."

I signaled the waiter and took two flutes. We toasted the President, said our goodbyes, and headed for the airport and a flight back to the real world.

Promoted to captain, July 1944. General Mark Clark pinning on the bars.

With my brother, Dale, and our
Republican standard-bearer, Barry Goldwater, in 1964.

Stu Spencer, political master strategist and my friend and adversary in the GOP presidential primary, in California, 1964.

University of Nebraska Board of Regents, 1966. I'm standing, far left. Second from the left, seated, is Chancellor Clifford Hardin, who became Secretary of Agriculture under President Richard Nixon.

Peg looks on as I'm sworn in to the US–Canada Boundary Commission at the State Department, November 1969.

Wielding the gavel at the Republican National Convention, Miami Beach, 1972.

With President Nixon at the White House,
press secretary Ron Ziegler in the background, 1972.

On the golf course with President
Gerald Ford, 1975.

Mabel "Dutch" Herman with her sons, Dick and Dale.

To Peg & Dick—
Dear & Cherished
friends—for all seasons!
Jan '83   Sincerely   Bob Strauss

Peg and me with our longtime friend, Bob Strauss, a Texan (and a Democrat), 1985.

With Secretary of State Jim Baker, who served three presidents and who,
in my opinion, would have made a great president himself.

With President George H. W. Bush at the White House, 1988.

Legendary Nebraska football coaches Tom Osborne (left) and Bob Devaney (right).
Together they brought the Big Red five national championships and
a tradition of high academic standards for the school's student athletes.

The next generation of Hermans:
Mike, Rick, Cathie, and Anne.

Dedicated in November 2012, the Dick and Peg Herman Family
Student Life Complex at the University of Nebraska. It was
Coach Tom Osborne's idea to add Peg's name to the student center.

VII.

The Nixon Years (2)
(1972–74)

MIAMI BEACH CONSIDERS LATE BID
GOP HINTS AT CONVENTION SITE SWITCH

—headline, *San Diego Evening Tribune*, April 19, 1972

It wasn't the sort of headline I was looking for when I'd answered the call to serve as Vice-Chairman of Arrangements for the 1972 Republican National Convention. The call had come from John Mitchell, the man in charge of the President's re-election campaign.

As Vice-Chairman of Arrangements, my job would be to plan and handle the logistics for a convention expected to draw some fifteen thousand people, including delegates, press, and guests.

On taking the job I contacted Don Ross, who'd handled arrangements for the 1968 convention. It wasn't the first time I'd followed Don's footsteps in holding a party position. A year before, I'd succeeded him as Republican National Committeeman for Nebraska when he moved on to a federal judgeship. On leaving, Don gave me one piece of advice:

"If anybody calls saying the White House wants this or that, tell them to put it in writing."

As it turned out, I had no problems with bureaucratic gadflies, my White House contact being Bill Timmons, whose skills as a political strategist and organizer would make my job easier. Nothing in Don's or Bill's experience, however, could have prepared me for the extraordinary problems that led up to the Republican National Convention of 1972.

★   ★   ★

To President Nixon, San Diego had always been his "lucky city." He'd carried it every election he'd ever run in. Add to that his feeling that incoming San Diego Mayor Pete Wilson was one of the GOP's bright young stars and it was clear to members of the site selection committee that there was but one option in choosing a city to hold the 1972 convention.

The question was whether San Diego, however lucky it had been for the President, was ready, willing, and able to host a national political convention at that time. San Diegans themselves were divided on the issue. The outgoing mayor, Frank Curran, had even told the press, "We need this like a hole in the head."

What Curran and other local opponents of hosting the convention were afraid of was their city's becoming a magnet for thousands of anti-war demonstrators of the kind that produced riots in Chicago at the Democratic National Convention four years earlier.

"Although San Diego did not have a history of violence and protests, local fears were not unfounded," wrote Richard Crawford in the *Journal of San Diego History* twenty years later. "Yippie leaders Abbie Hoffman and Jerry Rubin, two of the 'Chicago Seven' who led the riots in 1968, told the press they planned to lead a million protestors from all over the country into San Diego for the convention." (Another critic of the convention site, Florida GOP Chairman L.E. Thomas, commented that Hoffman and Rubin didn't have to recruit nationwide to raise that number since "there are more two-legged nuts per square acre in California than in any other part of the country.")

All that of course—policing the streets, curbing demonstrators, quelling riots—was outside my jurisdiction as Vice-Chairman of Arrangements. Before Hoffman, Rubin, and their followers could descend on San Diego, there had to be a convention in place—a hall to hold it and hotel space to accommodate thousands of visitors. And much as Pete Wilson and the party's host committee wanted it, local efforts to prepare San Diego for a national convention fell short.

The problem began with the limitations of the convention site, the city's Sports Arena. A good place to hold basketball games and circuses; but, as its operator, an aggressive Canadian entrepreneur named Peter Graham believed, no place to hold a Republican convention.

Excerpt, "When the Elephants Marched Out of San Diego," by Vincent S. Ancona, *Journal of San Diego History:*

Graham made clear his goal, "to get all I can, and if they don't like it, I'll lock the doors and they can go somewhere else."

The City of San Diego was helpless to do anything about Graham and the arena controversy. It held no power over the lessee of the arena and could not require Graham to do anything he didn't want to. Newly elected Mayor Pete Wilson offered his services as a mediator to Graham but he was flatly refused. The GOP also felt that they were at Graham's mercy. Although they had a contract with Graham, the convention was only a few months away, and any legal action would take months, if not years.

Getting it done had been my lifetime credo, from handling logistics during World War II through my years building a trucking company into a thriving business. No problem was beyond solving, as far as I was concerned, no obstacle so big I couldn't find a way around it. It went against my nature to throw up my hands and walk away from a problem. But however lucky San Diego had been for President Nixon in past elections, it didn't take long to conclude that as a convention site the city was a political disaster waiting to happen.

First, there were the limitations of Peter Graham's Sports Arena. We needed anywhere from six weeks to three months to prepare the place for an influx of fifteen thousand delegates and guests, and Graham would agree to give construction workers and technicians only two weeks to make the place convention-ready. Add to that the fact that while the cooling system in the arena was adequate for a sports crowd or circus, portable air conditioning would have to be brought in from Tennessee to deal with the heat generated by television and spot lighting. Overtime pay for workers trying to complete a three-month job in two weeks, the cost of hauling air conditioning cross-country—all this required money neither the city nor the GOP host committee had.

Not that our Peter Graham headaches stopped there: According to Leon Parma, chairman of the host committee, Graham was also demanding $500,000 in permanent improvements to his Sports Arena, including the construction of state-of-the-art television booths usable as press and VIP boxes after the convention. All these demands, he said, were "non-negotiable," and if we didn't like it we could go to . . .

"Keep trying," John Mitchell told me after I reported in on the problems we faced making San Diego our convention city. "The President wants it."

Try I would, but the day was fast coming when even Dick Nixon would give up on holding the convention in his "lucky city."

★   ★   ★

It would be money problems—not just the lack of it, but the source of original funding—that would finally end all hopes of making San Diego the site of the 1972 Republican National Convention.

Peter Graham's outlandish demands for his Sports Arena were a logistical nightmare, but the tipping point came with the news media's pouncing on a $400,000 pledge by International Telephone and Telegraph (ITT) as seed money to bring the convention to San Diego.

As the owner of two Sheraton hotels in San Diego and with a third under construction, ITT had an obvious stake in bringing a major convention to town. There was nothing illegal about that, but on being told of the $400,000 contribution my response was something other than the local host committee expected. "That's too much money coming from one source," I told them. "We don't want it."

I then issued a public statement rejecting the money, got on a plane headed for ITT headquarters in Boston, where I personally returned the uncashed check to ITT's Sheraton Hotel Group. All this took place months before columnist Jack Anderson broke the news that an internal ITT memorandum tied the contribution to a Justice Department antitrust investigation. A scandal in the making, but unmade by returning the check.

It's all there in the White House Watergate tapes: First, John Ehrlichman telling the President that because of my response there would be no negative blowback since "the Republican Party as such rejected the money"; then John Mitchell's backing that up with, "We won't have any trouble with the ITT gift because Herman returned it."

Check returned, ITT problem solved. But we still had the overall problem of finding a place to hold a national convention. With summer coming on, a decision had to be made. San Diego, for all its scenic attraction and the goodwill of the host committee, was out of the question. It was time to move to a place with greener, more welcome pastures.

*   *   *

After columnist Drew Pearson died and before Bob Woodward and Carl Bernstein broke open the Watergate scandal, Jack Anderson was the pre-eminent columnist in the country reporting behind-the-scenes political scandals.

It was Anderson who first reported the ITT contribution that put the final nail in any hope of San Diego's hosting our national convention. Then, going full circle, it was Anderson who broke the behind-the-scenes story of how the convention ended up in Miami Beach . . .

From *The Washington Post*, July 12, 1972
PARTIES RUN BIPARTISAN SHIP
by Jack Anderson

Miami Beach—While the parties bristle and brawl in the presidential campaign, they are cooperating secretly to make America's political processes work.

The Democrats, for example, quietly intervened to bring the homeless Republicans to Miami Beach when San Diego fell through as the GOP convention site.

The Republicans in return have scoured the countryside for office trailers at a rental rate the bankrupt Democrats can afford. On the QT, the Republicans have even helped the Democrats get ads for their convention program from GOP fat cats.

Their unusual cooperation springs from an amazing friendship between two political archrivals. They are GOP Vice Chairman Dick Herman, a conservative Omaha trucker, and financier Robert Strauss, the down-to-earth Democratic treasurer.

They have been conferring closely since February when they cautiously came together at Ford Motor headquarters in Washington to discuss corporate ads in the convention programs.

At first the two men circled each other like jungle cats. Then suddenly the impulsive Herman turned to their Ford hosts.

"Say, have you got a private room we could borrow for a moment?" While the motor men blinked, the two political rivals ducked into a private conference room and shut the door.

"Let's quit messing around, Bob," said Herman. "Let's get together and get something done."

"That's fine with me," said Strauss. He thrust out his hand and the two men shook.

Their first accomplishment was a joint telegram from Democratic Chairman Larry O'Brien and Republican Chairman Bob Dole, soliciting funds for the convention programs. The pair also brought together a dozen Democratic and Republican ad men to compare notes on how to meet their staggering convention costs . . .

The planning is now over, but Herman and Strauss are determined that their lesson in amity will not be forgotten. The two are proposing a bipartisan commission to study how cooperation can continue in the future to hold down the bankrupting costs of party conventions.

Not that Anderson, resourceful as he was, got the complete inside story. Left out was the key role John Connally played in getting me together with Bob Strauss.

Connally, the one-time Democratic governor of Texas and at that time Nixon's Secretary of Treasury, had learned of the situation in San Diego. Calling from his home in Texas, his opening words were, "I understand you're having problems. I'm having dinner with someone who might be of help." He put Strauss on the line.

I knew Strauss by reputation as a Texan who headed one of the most influential law firms in Washington. As Democratic Party treasurer at the time, he was involved in putting together that year's Democratic national convention in Miami, scheduled to take place a few weeks before ours.

Strauss took the phone. After a few minutes' banter, we set up a meeting in Washington. To borrow the line from one of my favorite wartime movies, it was the beginning of a beautiful friendship. I would work with Bob and his fellow Texan George Bristol through the summer in what Jack Anderson rightly called "a lesson in amity."

But first, there was the matter of giving John Mitchell the news. . . .

**Excerpt, long-distance telephone conversation between
Dick Herman and John Mitchell, June 10, 1972**

HERMAN: John, I've made a decision to move the convention.
We're headed for Miami. If I don't hear from you in thirty minutes, I'm on my way.

MITCHELL: Don't you think you ought to tell Bob Dole?

Good idea. Senator Dole, after all, was the Convention Chairman. I
reached him in New Orleans, where he was scheduled to speak at Loyola
University. Our conversation was brief and cordial. I went over our problems and told him time was running out on our holding the convention
in San Diego.

BOB DOLE: It's your call, Dick. Move it.

Next step, boarding a plane to Miami and an emergency meeting
with the city council.

*　　*　　*

The obvious advantage of moving the convention to where the
Democrats were holding theirs was that most of the logistical problems had already been solved: The Convention Center was already
wired, the broadcast booth in place. We knew there were more than
enough hotel rooms available, and we also knew that an inland water
system separated the Center from the city, making crowd control more
manageable.

In short, everything fell into place—except for the Miami council's
reluctance to our holding our convention in their city. All that members
of the council could see were hordes of antiwar demonstrators descend-
ing on south Florida, disrupting the summer tourist trade. It would take
a midnight meeting with Jerris Leonard of the Justice Department and a

pledge of $44 million for extra security for *both* conventions, Democratic and Republican, to get their approval.

At long last we had a workable convention site where we could take on the relatively simple task of getting thousands of delegates assembled, housed, and ready to nominate a national ticket for the 1972 presidential campaign.

★   ★   ★

It was a convention of firsts: Anne Armstrong of Texas became the first woman to deliver a keynote address at a national political convention, Republican or Democratic; Pat Nixon would be the first First Lady to address a national convention since Eleanor Roosevelt spoke at the Democratic convention in 1944.

The only disruption involving security came on the last night, when a group of demonstrators gathered in front of the Center and police had to disperse them with tear gas. Fortunately, there was no violence and the area was cleared without casualties.

Otherwise things went according to schedule, allowing for the routine delays and glitches that came with the handling of thousands of political convention-goers. The national ticket was set—Nixon-Agnew, running on the slogan NOW MORE THAN EVER—and there were no major intraparty disputes to settle.

To say that I breathed a sigh of relief Friday morning, with delegates headed for home and the convention floor being cleared, would be an understatement. In truckers' language, it had been a long haul since that day I'd arrived in San Diego to set up convention arrangements. A long haul, but one I now look back on as the most rewarding journey in a lifetime of political travels.

★   ★   ★

From *Omaha World-Herald*, August 21, 1972
NEBRASKANS CARRY FOOTBALL,
SONG TO GOP CONVENTION
By Don Walton

Miami Beach—Omaha brought a football and the strains of "There Is No Place Like Nebraska" to the Republican National Convention Monday.

The football, provided by Omaha Councilman Warren Swigart, was attached to Nebraska's convention hall banner, a symbol of the Cornhuskers' number one status.

The tune was provided by the Ray Bloch Orchestra in tribute to Dick Herman of Omaha, who put together the arrangements for the GOP convention.

"They said it couldn't be done, there's no way," Republican National Chairman Bob Dole told the opening session of the convention in describing Herman's task of arranging the big conclave. "But here we are today and we have Dick Herman to thank for it."

Thanks to be shared with a first-class staff that helped in handling the big decisions and myriad details that go into the making of a successful national convention: Jim Gale, a former FBI man and an expert on security matters, was invaluable in spotting and heading off problems along the way, from San Diego to Miami; Paul Wagner, a fellow Nebraskan who'd served in the Eisenhower White House and as Barry Goldwater's press secretary, who took on the headache of dealing with hundreds of print, TV, and radio journalists clamoring for attention; and Dan Sullivan, a bright, energetic young man with a gift for smoothing out rough patches and getting things done.

★   ★   ★

The celebration of President Nixon's election-day victory at Washington's Shoreham hotel that November was subdued compared with the one that had taken place four years earlier at the Waldorf Astoria hotel in New York. There were cheers all around as the state-by-state results came in, but no sense of excitement since, for the first time, Dick Nixon was involved in a presidential race that wasn't a nail-biter.

It was a landslide win, the Democratic ticket of George McGovern and Sargent Shriver losing by the biggest margin since FDR defeated Alf Landon in 1936. The Democrats had come into the 1972 campaign a divided party, the old Roosevelt coalition torn apart by the rise of a radical new left and the falling away of the once-Solid South.

All of which made the heavy-handed overkill of Watergate hard to comprehend. Not only was it criminal, it was politically stupid. Given the condition of the Democratic opposition in 1972, there was no way President Nixon could have failed to be re-elected and nothing in DNC Chairman Larry O'Brien's Watergate files could have helped or hurt the President's campaign.

Four decades later those of us who supported Dick Nixon still have no answer to the question of how a man as politically astute as he could have allowed, much less approved, the Watergate break-in. But this much I know: John Mitchell neither instigated nor authorized that lawless operation. As all the records (including the White House tapes) show, Watergate was wholly the product of those members of the President's staff who, in the words of John Dean, were "blinded by ambition."

It was Dean, the lead witness in the Senate Watergate hearings, who later would tell a reporter, "The John Mitchell I know is far different from the man the public perceives. I don't look upon Mitchell as a sinister force. . . . I saw him more as a restraining influence on Nixon and some of the people in the Nixon White House."

A broken man, John Mitchell lived out his last years in Washington with serious health problems. As biographer James Rosen describes John's life after Watergate, "The Wall Street wizard who once commanded the respect of the Rockefellers was now a disbarred ex-convict, his opportunities limited." He would die of a heart attack on a Georgetown street on November 9, 1988, with the *Washington Post* running an obituary that summed him up as

> the ultimate Nixon loyalist. Unlike some of his codefendants, Mitchell wrote no memoir, no kiss-and-tell insider report, no novelized version of his life in Washington. He lived according to his own code and to the end of his Watergate ordeal, he was a stand-up guy.

That fit perfectly my own impression and memory of John. Asked by my friend Mike Yanney whether, on looking back, he had any regrets in life, the Strong Man thought awhile, then said, "Yes, that I wasn't there when the president needed me the most."[1]

An added note about my friendship with John Mitchell: On his release from prison John disappeared from public view, refusing even to contact old associates. Bob Mardian commented on this at a dinner gathering one evening, stating flatly that "John won't go out." I picked up a phone, called our old friend and told him that if he didn't join us for dinner I'd have a fire rescue squad at his residency the following night. I'd also have a car to pick him up—he could take his choice.

That broke the ice. John joined Bob, Dick Kleindienst, and me the following evening, we had a great time telling old political war stories, and closed out the restaurant. It was the first of an annual John Mitchell Dinner I sponsored until his death in November 1988. A year later I hosted a tribute dinner to John—this one, at my suggestion, with former President Nixon as our guest.

★　　　★　　　★

While the news media focused on the Watergate investigation, events in the Middle East were bringing our national economy to a standstill. After Egypt, Syria, and Jordan launched the Yom Kippur War against Israel in October 1973, the Arabs' Organization of the Petroleum

Exporting Countries (OPEC) placed an embargo on shipments of oil to all countries allied with Israel.

Within days, lines formed outside filling stations across the country. At one New Jersey site, a line was reported as more than four miles long. With the Department of Transportation (DOT) overwhelmed, President Nixon appointed William Simon as energy czar, charged with handling demands for fuel.

I knew Bill Simon as one of the nation's smartest businessmen, but it soon became obvious that his expertise didn't extend to the field of transportation.

Calling on my experience with fuel allocations during World War II, I flew to Washington to meet with Simon, laying out a plan that gave fuel priority to the most essential segments of the economy. The plan was simplicity itself. Major fuel users would certify their needs to DOT regional depots across the country and draw their requisitions.

Simon, quick to see the feasibility of the plan, signed off on it and thanked me for making his job easier. His political star, it soon became apparent, was on the rise. Within a year, he would be appointed Secretary of Treasury.

★   ★   ★

VIII.

The Underrated:
Jerry and George
(1974–1992)

Our long national nightmare is over.

—President Ford, August 9, 1974

No president in American history—not Lincoln in 1861, not Roosevelt in 1933, not Truman in 1945—entered the White House under a greater handicap than Gerald Ford in 1974. The executive office was under a dark cloud, public confidence in government was near an all-time low, and the incoming president lacked not only a mandate but a popular vote electing him to national office.

To add to that handicap, Ford was inaccurately portrayed by Washington political pundits as having been a mediocre Member of Congress with nothing in his years of service that qualified him for higher office. Because he'd played football at the University of Michigan, he was unfairly characterized as an affable jock with no intellectual depth.

Nothing could be further from the truth. You don't work your way through the University of Michigan on the way to an economics degree, then graduate in the top 25 percent of your class at Yale Law School, without a first-class mind and the ability to excel.

Like other heartland members of the Republican National Committee, I was saddened by President Nixon's having to resign his office but pleased to see Jerry, a fellow Midwesterner, succeed him; though, I have to admit, less than pleased when Nelson Rockefeller was chosen to step in as vice president.

Memories of Rockefeller's bitter campaigns against Goldwater in 1964 and Nixon in 1968 were still with me. Added to that, I had what I thought was the ideal choice for the vice presidency, George Bush.

As Chairman of the RNC during the darkest days of the Watergate scandal, George had stayed cool and focused, never losing sight of the party's—or more important, the country's—best interests. His record as a Member of Congress and U.S. Ambassador to the United Nations gave him a range of experience needed in the person next in line to the presidency.

Along with other members of the National Committee I lobbied hard for George, but made the mistake of not talking directly to the President himself. Ford's choice, Rockefeller, though well-received on the East Coast, drew criticism among rank-and-file party members in the South and Midwest who regarded the New York governor as a liberal millionaire out of touch with anything west of the Hudson River.

Looking ahead to 1976, I felt President Ford's decision regarding Rockefeller was a mistake. In the biggest decision made in his first days in office, however—the Nixon pardon—I felt Ford, whatever the cost in political terms, made not only the right but the courageous choice.

I shudder to think of the consequences that would have followed if the country had been subjected to the public trial of an ex-president, a process that could have gone on for months if not years—a three-ring media circus in the midst of a Cold War overseas and an economic crisis here at home. But though the Nixon pardon was right in terms of the good of the country, it had a negative impact on Ford's poll numbers.

Not that the public's disapproval of the pardon was the only handicap the new President would have to overcome to win the office in his own right. In addition to the ongoing war in Vietnam, the national economy was suffering from the combined impact of a recession and hyperinflation. It was a steep political hill for Jerry Ford to climb in 1976 but I was determined to help him climb it.

One way to help was to join the administration's effort to upgrade the efficiency of the country's troubled transportation industry. Appointed a public member of the National Transportation Policy Study Commission, I worked with other members—six U.S. Senators, six Congressmen, and five other public members—to free the industry from outdated regulations that gave unions like the Teamsters and International Longshoremen power enough to shut down the country. The Commission's work proved to be the first step in an ongoing program of deregulation in trucking, railroad, airline, and water transportation.

⋆   ⋆   ⋆

Attending meetings of the Commission in Washington gave me an opportunity to stay in touch with President Ford's campaign team. There was no doubt I'd play a role in the 1976 campaign. The only question was how big a role.

One possibility, put forward by Dean Burch, was to become Chairman of the National Committee for the Election of President Ford. Dean, who'd served as RNC Chairman during the Goldwater campaign, called me in Omaha to say I was the President's choice for the job. It was flattering, but as Adlai Stevenson once said, "Flattery is all right, if you don't inhale."

My first response, after thinking it over, was to call Dean back and accept. Luckily, I couldn't get him on the line. After a sleepless night rethinking that decision, I concluded that the total commitment the job would require—away for home, away from business—was more than I could make in the coming year. When I got Dean on the phone the next morning, I told him I couldn't take on the chairmanship but was ready to go to work on a lesser assignment. As it turned out, my decision proved no loss to the Ford campaign. When Jim Baker took over as campaign manager and Stu Spencer stepped in as political director, I knew that Jerry Ford's campaign to win the party's nomination and election in 1976 was in the best of hands.

★   ★   ★

Dean's offer was the second in a year to tempt me into a full-scale commitment to political life. The first came from friends in the RNC in the early months of 1974. The support was there and the money could be raised, they told me, if I decided to run for governor of Nebraska. The state chairman of the party was all for it, along with other community leaders I'd worked with.

More flattery, but again I opted not to inhale. Politics, as Peg was the first to point out, had always been my avocation, my way of giving back for the success I'd been able to achieve as a businessman. It was best, I decided (with Peg's help), to leave it that way.

Too bad in one respect: Peg would have made a marvelous First Lady of Nebraska.

★   ★   ★

July 4, 1976. It was an invitation you didn't decline. Peg and I were never drawn to the lure of Washington social life, but a bicentennial White House dinner honoring Queen Elizabeth would be something to tell our grandchildren about.

Not that the trip, coming little more than a month before the Party's national convention, would be purely social in nature. The Kansas City convention would go on record as being the last, Republican or Democratic, in which the presidential nominee hadn't been determined before the convention began.

It was a two-man race, right from the beginning, and before it was over neither candidate felt very kindly toward the other. Since leaving the California governorship two years earlier, Ronald Reagan had set his sights on the White House, running as a conservative candidate in the mold of Barry Goldwater.

Goldwater himself, though he respected Reagan, was lined up behind President Ford. Republicans, said Barry, don't turn their backs on incumbents of their own party (as Democrats had done to Lyndon Johnson in 1968). Add to that the fact that the last thing the party needed after Watergate was a divisive fight for the nomination. Unfortunately, that was exactly what took place, from the early primaries on into the convention itself.

The President took an early lead in the delegate count after winning New Hampshire and the early primaries. But Reagan, backed by Senator Jesse Helms, had come back with an upset win in North Carolina. The winning issue: Reagan's opposition to ceding the Panama Canal to the Panamanians. As Craig Shirley wrote in his history of the 1976 campaign, *Reagan's Revolution*:

> Reagan, in speech after speech, would make his case for keeping the Canal, usually thundering, "It's ours! We built it! We paid for it! And we should keep it!"

Reagan's criticism of Ford's foreign policy didn't stop with the Canal issue, however. The old divide between those who favored détente with the Soviet Union and those wanting a more assertive Cold War policy came back into play. As a leading advocate of détente, Secretary of State Henry Kissinger was the lightning rod on this issue, and Reagan's strategy team, headed by John Sears, hoped to swing the convention its way by making Kissinger's foreign policy a key issue.

Anticipating a floor fight on the foreign policy plank of the party platform, some Ford strategists, including Bill Timmons, wanted to turn the tables on Reagan and Sears by changing the convention rules in Kansas City. Their idea was to have the delegates debate and vote on the party platform *after*, rather than before, the presidential nomination.

Along with others called in to plan convention strategy, I opposed the rules change, arguing that it ran against not only tradition but common sense to nominate a candidate without his knowing the party's position on the issues. As a conservative, I felt that reversing the order of business for tactical reasons was wrong, both as a matter of principle and practicality. The resentment it would cause among Reagan supporters could lead them to sit on their hands during the campaign. We needed a united party to win in November.

The issue was decided in favor of not changing the rules in a top-level strategy meeting at the White House. One by one those like Timmons, who favored the rules change, and those of us who opposed it, offered our cases. The President heard us out, then made his decision, going over the arguments made by each of us.

There's a point to be made here about the qualities of leadership. We generally think of our leaders in the White House in terms of their ability to speak, to persuade, as Teddy Roosevelt put it, from "the bully pulpit." But there's another side of true leadership that's less noted but equally important—the ability to listen. Jerry Ford had that quality. At a later time, Bill Scranton, the former governor of Pennsylvania who served as Ford's U.N. Ambassador, told me that the only President he'd known with the same ability to hear all sides, to listen patiently before making a decision, was Dwight Eisenhower.

I think Ike, with his strict military background, would have come down the same way President Ford did on whether to change the convention rules—against the idea. We'll take our chances on a convention floor fight over foreign policy, Ford told us. The rules will stay as they are. First the vote on the platform, then the nomination.

Four years earlier Bill Timmons and I had crossed swords over an issue at the convention in Miami. That one he won. Coming out of the White House after Ford's decision against a rules change, Bill clapped me on the back, nodded, and said, "This one's yours. Now we're even."

★   ★   ★

KANSAS CITY, MO., August 16–19, 1976

This would be my sixth national convention, twenty years having passed since I'd worked the phones and carried messages during the 1956 gathering that renominated President Eisenhower. Though still in my middle years, I could gauge the passage of time by the new faces around me, relative youngsters like Dick Cheney and Jim Baker, who were running things for the Ford campaign as the fight for delegates reached its climax.

Cheney had taken over as White House chief of staff after Donald Rumsfeld left that job to become Secretary of Defense. Baker had been Assistant Secretary of Commerce and was called in to become Ford's campaign manager in a staff shake-up aimed at re-energizing the President's campaign. Working together—as they would a decade and a half later, when Cheney was George H. W. Bush's Secretary of Defense and Baker was Secretary of State—they were the key players in the drive to gather the 1,130 voting delegates the President needed to win the nomination.

As a Ford floor manager, I came to know Jim Baker as a gentleman, a scholar, and one of the most astute young political minds in either party. It came as no surprise when years later he rose to become White House chief of staff and Secretary of Treasury under President Reagan, then Secretary of State under President George H. W. Bush.

It was Jim who took the lead in negotiating a foreign policy plank in the 1976 platform that helped avoid a bitter party split, and Jim who outmaneuvered Reagan strategist John Sears to defeat a rules change that would have required Ford to name his vice presidential choice before voting began on the presidential nomination.

The vote was on Rule 16-C, and Sears, according to news reports at the time, saw it as a make-or-break opportunity to swing Southern delegates from Ford to Reagan. Nelson Rockefeller had announced earlier that he wouldn't run for vice president in the fall and half a dozen prospects were being touted for the job. It was Sears' hope that by naming one, Ford would alienate all the others, and their supporters would defect to Reagan in the vote for the presidential nomination.[1]

Sears' rule change was rejected in a test vote that signaled how the final vote for the presidential nomination would turn out. It was close, but Ford was nominated, and the party, despite all differences, held together. The only question left was who the vice presidential nominee would be.

★   ★   ★

I'd hoped that the second time around Jerry Ford might recognize the mistake he'd made by not naming George Bush as his vice presidential choice when he first took office. Much like the president, George had been continually underrated by those who mistook a lack of political bluster for weakness.

Anyone who looked at George's record would know otherwise. At age seventeen, he volunteered for service after Pearl Harbor and became the youngest aviator in the Navy, winning the Distinguished Flying Cross after being shot down in the Pacific. Returning home after the war, he built a successful oil business in Texas, then went on to become Houston's first Republican congressman, facing down racist opposition back home when he voted for the Open Housing Bill. As U.S. Ambassador to the United Nations, Chairman of the RNC, envoy to China, and head of the CIA, George had made a name for himself as a man who took on tough assignments and got things done.

Then there were the pure political arguments in favor of a Ford-Bush ticket. The President needed a running mate who would not only appeal to independent voters but breach the gap between Midwest and Southern conservatives and the Eastern wing of the party. Though a Texan, George's roots were in New England, where his father, Prescott, had served as Connecticut's senior U.S. senator during the Eisenhower years.

To those who had followed his career and witnessed his leadership when he chaired the Republican National Committee during the party's Watergate crisis, George was the logical choice for the vice presidential nomination in 1976. Why President Ford didn't see that remains one of the mysteries of my many years in politics. And with due respect to my friend and fellow Midwesterner Bob Dole, I'm convinced that had George rather than Bob been on the ticket that year, the outcome in November would have been different.

That said, the political gods keep their own schedule. George's time, though overdue, was coming—as was Ronald Reagan's.

★ ★ ★

DETROIT, July 14–17, 1980

MAKE AMERICA GREAT AGAIN

—Campaign slogan, 1980 Republican national ticket

George Bush went into the fight for the 1980 Republican presidential nomination as a decided underdog. Or, as he put it, "an asterisk in the Gallup poll." There were others I could have backed at the time— Reagan, Dole, Howard Baker, John Connally—but none, in my opinion, measured up to George in terms of experience and ability. I was there when he announced his candidacy at the National Press Club in the spring of 1979 and traveled with him on his first campaign trip to New Hampshire.

The media paid little attention to Bush's candidacy at the time. One political column dismissed it as "a campaign that peaked before it was even announced." But the Washington pundits overlooked two factors in George's favor: First, he was a tireless campaigner with bulldog tenacity; second, he had the best campaign manager in the business, Jim Baker, a political strategist always two steps ahead of the competition.

To the Washington pundits, the race for the 1980 Republican presidential nomination was seen as Reagan against the field. When Bush came out of nowhere to win the Iowa caucuses, it turned into a two-way race, with all the other candidates—Dole, Howard Baker, Connally—dropping out one by one. Though George himself had to concede defeat after Reagan won enough delegates to secure the nomination, he had been the last man standing and went into the convention at Detroit, once again, as the logical choice for the vice presidential nomination.

For a while it appeared that the old jinx that had worked against him three times before was at it again. With Henry Kissinger and Donald Rumsfeld in the lead, a small group of Washington insiders with their own agenda came up with the idea of a "Dream Ticket" of Ronald Reagan for President and Jerry Ford for Vice President. That Ford would even entertain the idea surprised me, but he was persuaded that if details could be worked out, a Reagan-Ford partnership would be best for the party and the country.

As I saw it, the notion of a Reagan-Ford ticket was, first of all, unworkable. Running into George Romney, who was pushing the idea on the convention floor, I told him as much by asking a simple question: "You were Chairman of American Motors at one time, weren't you?" When he answered yes, I asked him another: "How would you like to go back as vice-chairman?"

The second problem I saw with the so-called "Dream Ticket" was the strong possibility it would alienate conservatives who'd see the possible return of Henry Kissinger as Secretary of State as a good reason to stay home on Election Day.

In time, all this became clear to both major players in the "Dream Ticket" scenario. After a late-night meeting, both Reagan and Ford agreed it wouldn't work. But not before George Bush, having been disappointed three times in the past, had all but given up hope he'd become the vice presidential nominee.

Coming off the podium after a speech to the convention, George was in a mood I'd never seen him in before—downbeat and depressed. It seemed the old jinx had worked again and there was nothing to be done about it.

Jim Baker thought otherwise, however, and so did I. There were those

in the Reagan inner circle—Lyn Nofziger, Ed Meese, Dick Wirthlin—
who could look at the poll numbers and tell that George Bush would
bring more to the national ticket than anyone else. Their idea of a "Dream
Ticket" was one that would put Ronald Reagan in the White House
with the strongest possible running mate: Reagan-Bush it would be.

Throughout his political career, critics—mostly Democrats—made
the mistake of dismissing Ronald Reagan as a mere actor, good only at
reading cue cards. Political history tells us otherwise. Reagan was one of
the shrewdest politicians of his time and not only his choice of George
Bush as his running mate, but the dramatic way he announced it—a
late-night convention speech that brought the crowd to its feet—proved
that. It not only broke the tension but unified the party.

I was there when Reagan's two deputies, Dick Allen and Marty
Anderson, along with a swarm of Secret Service agents, showed up at
the Bush suite at the Pontchartrain Hotel to confirm the good news. For
George and his family, it was time for a celebration. The jinx had finally
been broken.

★   ★   ★

*[Bush] was, as his friend [Jim] Baker said years later, a "model vice
president." He was dedicated, energetic, and loyal; the subordinate
who left no doubt about his selfless devotion to the cause. No longer
was the vice presidency worth "a pitcher of warm spit," in John Nance
Garner's inelegant phrase; it had muscle, political and statutory.
They combined to make the vice presidency a part of presidential
administrations in ways the Founding Fathers had not envisioned.*

**—from Herbert S. Parmet's *George Bush:*
*The Life of a Lone Star Yankee***

John Nance Garner's description of the importance of the vice presidency
may have been accurate at one time, but things changed dramatically

after the Hoover Commission upgraded the office in 1949. No longer was the vice president simply presiding officer of the U.S. Senate. He became an integral part of the executive branch, sitting in on meetings of the Cabinet, the National Security Council, and the Domestic Council. Given that experience, every vice president since Dick Nixon in 1960 has had a head start in running for the White House when his time came.

George Bush's time came in 1988, and though he faced tough opposition in the primaries—Bob Dole being his chief opponent—his years of service as Ronald Reagan's loyal vice president earned him the party's presidential nomination at the New Orleans convention in July.

It was then that George made what I considered at the time—and still do, a quarter-century later—the biggest mistake of his political life.

*   *   *

The New Orleans convention of 1988 was the first in thirty years I didn't attend. No longer the National Committeeman from Nebraska—Peg and I had moved to California years earlier—I watched from a distance as George took over leadership of the party.

Truth was, I didn't miss the hurly-burly of late-night strategy meetings and delegate counts one bit. Even when politics is only an avocation, there comes a time when a party elder—and after eight conventions I qualified as such—should step back to make room for new faces and new ideas.

I think George Bush had something like that in mind when he made his decision as to who would be his running mate in the 1988 presidential election. Our generation—the World War II generation—had seen our day and it was time to pass the torch to the postwar Baby Boomers.

Theoretically, that was the right idea—provided he picked the right man for the job, someone qualified by experience and temperament to take over the reins of government should something happen to the president.

Why George decided Dan Quayle fit that description is something I'll never understand. Any way I looked at it, the idea of Vice President Quayle, next in line for the White House, left me shaking my head.

Not that I was the only strong Bush supporter who saw the choice of Quayle as a monumental mistake. Other members of George's inner circle of friends and advisors thought the same. But Bush-Quayle it would be, and much as I felt George Bush was the man best qualified to lead the nation as we headed into the 1990s, my faith was shaken by what I considered a failure in judgment in the first decision he made as a presidential nominee.

As I first told Peg—and then Jim Baker—the days and weeks following the convention became a time for soul-searching. There was no way, hard as I'd worked for George in the past, that I could conscientiously take part in any campaign that would place a man I considered completely unqualified only one heartbeat away from the presidency. The issue was personal and the question I had to answer was, *What do I do come Election Day?*

★　　　★　　　★

Sometimes party loyalty asks too much.

—John F. Kennedy, on refusing to nominate a Democrat he considered unqualified to the federal bench (1961)

The term "maverick" has been overused and misused in recent years, but coming from Nebraska, I always thought of it as another term for independent thinker. I grew up at a time when our senior Republican U.S. Senator, George Norris, was bucking the party establishment by not only backing but spearheading New Deal legislation to create the Tennessee Valley Authority—not because it helped him politically, but because he thought it was the right thing to do.

Whatever role I played as a party official, I always weighed issues on what I considered their merits, not according to some rigid political doctrine. Fortunately, I've been blessed with friends who recognized that, never letting whatever political differences we had stand in the way of our friendship.

A few days after the election in November 1988, I came to Washington and called Jim Baker's office at the White House to set up a meeting. He suggested we have lunch, either in the White House Mess or in his office. I opted for the office, since I wanted our meeting to be private and uninterrupted. It didn't take long after I'd arrived to get around to the subject on both our minds.

"So," Jim asked after we'd spent a few minutes in small talk, "how did you finally end up voting?"

Needless to say, I was ready for the question, spelling out not only my misgivings about Dan Quayle's serving as vice president, but the prospect that he'd be in line for the presidential nomination after George left office. I'd voted, I said, for the first time in my life, the Democratic ticket.

Jim didn't change expression, or say a thing. Our lunch was ready, and as a table was rolled into the office we sat down together. Finally, Jim spoke up.

"Dick," he said, "I have four tickets to the Alfalfa Club dinner,[2] and I know you haven't been in a couple of years. Why don't you join me?"

As far as Jim was concerned, our conversation about the election was over. We never discussed it again. As I say, a gentleman, a scholar, and a friend to this day.

★   ★   ★

Returning home to Omaha from California in 1996, I was often asked whether I'd renew my active role in state and national politics. There was no chance of that, however. The political game—and that's what it had become, more a game than a public service—was changing in ways I didn't care for.

Money has always been important in campaigns and elections, but by the mid-1990s, running for even a minor office required candidates to spend more time in fundraising than exploring the issues. The stakes had become so high for candidates and their financial contributors that a mean-spirited personal tone seemed to enter every campaign, from local school board elections to Congress and the presidency.

Not that I cut off all my political ties. There were too many friends still active in Lincoln and Washington to do that. Travels were frequent, and once a year I'd go to Washington to host the John Mitchell Dinner, a gathering of all those, young and old, who knew and remembered John as a great American whose friendship we cherished.

For the most part, however, my time and resources went into local and regional causes, like the Don't Smoke Program for youngsters at Sacred Heart School in North City, Iowa, one of Peg's favorites that became a model project for several schools around the country.

My one favorite? Anyone who spent five minutes in the Herman household wouldn't have to ask. The memorabilia, in Big Red and White, is everywhere, reflecting not just an avocation but a lifetime commitment . . .

★   ★   ★

IX.

Once a Husker . . .

I flew out to Nebraska to watch as an entire state went bananas over football. Ranchers rode in from three hundred miles away, dressed all in red, they and their wives, and they painted the town the same color. At two in the afternoon on a Saturday the stadium was a pulsating red mass. Once I stopped at a town in the remote southwest corner of the state, and the local bank had purchased a monstrous billboard to proclaim, "Go Big Red." I took the trouble to stop by the bank and ask why a business four hundred miles from the university would be so excited about football, and the banker said, "Our clients take it for granted that we're solvent. But if they suspected for even one minute that we were not sound where Big Red is concerned, they'd drive me out of business."

—from *Sports in America* by James A. Michener (1976)

★   ★   ★

To keep the record straight, it's not all about football. It's true we Nebraskans are proud of our university's five national football championships, but we're equally proud of our three Nobel Prize winners, our eight Pulitzer Prize winners, and our twenty-two Rhodes Scholar students.

Still, as a sage observer of human nature once said, you don't bring 90,000-plus fans to campus on Saturday afternoons in the fall to see a mathematics exam. Sports, as James Michener wrote after traveling the country forty years ago, is the tie that binds Americans to their communities and keeps alumni in touch with their alma maters.

In Nebraska, a state with only one major university campus and no professional sports team, that tie is especially binding. As Chancellor of the University of Nebraska in the early 1960s, Cliff Hardin saw the need to fill Memorial Stadium on Saturday afternoons in the fall as an important part of his job.

Cliff was at heart an academic. But as Chancellor he worked to enhance the school's reputation not only in agricultural studies but on the football field. While he upgraded the faculty by increasing professors' pay, he also sought to upgrade the football team after a series of poor seasons.

The key to success in any field, as I've said, is finding the right people for the right jobs. Cliff had come to Nebraska from Michigan State, where he'd known Duffy Daugherty, one of the best football coaches in the country at the time. He tried to lure Daugherty to Lincoln, without success. But Daugherty had a recommendation: If Nebraska wanted a winner, he said, put in a call to Bob Devaney at the University of Wyoming. The call was made. Devaney and his staff took over the Huskers, and within a year Nebraska was playing in the Orange Bowl (Huskers 13, Auburn 7).

Bob would go on to win back-to-back national championships (1970–71), eight conference titles, and nine bowl games before moving on to become Nebraska's Athletic Director in 1972. He was succeeded by his top assistant, Tom Osborne, who carried on the winning tradition (three national championships, thirteen conference titles, and the best five-year winning run in collegiate history).

As a coach and educator (a Ph.D. in Educational Psychology), Tom saw beyond making his players winners on the football field. He wanted them to be winners in life as well, to leave school with something more than championship rings. What he had in mind was the building of a student life complex—a state-of-the-art study center for Nebraska athletes in all sports.

It was a vision that I, along with my brother Dale, not only shared but would lend every effort to make a reality.

★   ★   ★

It was as a member of the university Board of Regents that I first came to know and appreciate Tom Osborne's focus on setting high academic standards for Nebraska's student-athletes. I was elected a Regent in 1966 and served four years, resigning only after becoming Nebraska's Republican National Committeeman. Since the Board was by law non-partisan, I thought it best to avoid any idea that politics might play a part in any decision I made as a Regent.

Though no longer a Regent, I still remained active in alumni affairs. Peg and I could be counted on to join the Big Red crowd at Memorial Stadium on football weekends and spend our winter holidays traveling to Miami, New Orleans, or wherever the Huskers' post-season bowl schedule might take us.

My involvement as a Nebraska alumnus didn't end there, however. There was a debt I owed the University of Nebraska for what it had given me many years before, when I was a small-town youth, a country boy whose first real contact with the outside world was the welcoming campus at Lincoln.

★   ★   ★

In 1989, Dale and I endowed an annual banquet honoring Nebraska athletes in all sports who have excelled in their studies with a 3.0 or higher grade point average. A special honor called the Herman Award is given to the Nebraska athletic teams, both men's and women's, that achieve the highest grade point average among all Husker teams each year. With relatives and friends in attendance, the banquet in recent years has hosted some eight hundred to nine hundred proud members of the Husker family.

It was Tom Osborne who provided the inspiration and guidance for the awards banquet. And it was Tom, as both a coach and an educator, who took the lead in bringing about a student center that two decades later would serve to make Nebraska student-athletes high achievers in the classroom as well as on the playing field.

★   ★   ★

Dick Herman and his late brother Dale had a vision in 1989 to have our athletic department become the national leader in academics, and because of their generosity their vision has come true.

—Dennis Leblanc, Nebraska's Senior Associate Athletic Director for Academics, November 10, 2012

Peg and Dale had been gone for ten years, but in my heart I know they were with me the day the ceremony took place that opened the new academic center in the West Lobby of Memorial Stadium.

They were there, looking down, when the ribbon was cut and Harvey Perlman, the University Chancellor, spoke of the academic success of Nebraska student-athletes, adding, "I don't think we could have been so successful for as long as we have without Dick and Peg Herman and their family."

It was Tom Osborne's idea to add Peg's name to the center. As Coach and then Athletic Director, Tom knew the role she had played in making it possible. For sixty-one years Peg and I were together in everything I'd undertaken, whether in business, politics, or alumni affairs.

Sixty-one years of lifetime partnership; which is why I know she was there that day and has been there every day since, if only in spirit, as young Nebraska student-athletes in all sports walk through the portals under the nameplate of the

DICK AND PEG HERMAN
FAMILY STUDENT LIFE COMPLEX

★   ★   ★

It was the comedian Jackie Gleason in a serious moment who said that while there's no such thing as a Fountain of Youth, if you're lucky you grow old with fond memories.

Lord knows I've been lucky. Fond memories abound, and none so fond as those Peg and I shared of Saturday afternoons in the fall on the campus at Lincoln as we joined family and friends to cheer the Huskers on. Yet the game that first comes to mind after all these years is the one between Nebraska and Oklahoma at Memorial Stadium, November 23, 1963. An unhappy moment in history for those old enough to remember—a weekend unlike any experienced by Americans in the 20th century.

The day before, I'd been busy closing out the annual meeting of the Nebraska State Chamber of Commerce and Industry in Omaha. As president, I was called to the phone for an urgent message: President Kennedy had been shot in Dallas.

Needless to say, the last thing on anyone's mind as the meeting adjourned was the football weekend members had planned around the Nebraska–Oklahoma game the next day. There was a question as to whether it would even take place. But Bud Wilkinson, the legendary Oklahoma coach, was a friend of the Kennedy family and among those who thought that, if anything, President Kennedy and his brother Bob would want the game played. And so it was.

Of the many—literally hundreds—of games that Peg and I attended at Memorial Stadium in a half-century, the one that took place that Saturday in November stands out like no other. The stadium was filled to capacity, as usual. All the trappings—bands, cheerleaders, mascots—were on hand, as usual. Players on both teams played their hearts out, as usual. But nothing else was as usual.

The Nebraska–Oklahoma rivalry in those years was one of the most heated in the country. On any other Husker–Sooner game day the focus would have been on which team would, at the final whistle, be headed for a national championship or big bowl game. On that day, however, who won or lost seemed less important than the need for the country to come together, as it had in other moments of national tragedy, one people united.

As those who knew the fallen President best could tell us, that was the way John F. Kennedy would have wanted it.

★   ★   ★

AS I REMEMBER
by Tom Osborne

Few, if any, fans have done as much for University of Nebraska Athletics as Dick Herman and his family. Dick was elected to the University of Nebraska Board of Regents in 1966 and took a great interest in the University as a whole but was particularly interested in Athletics. He got to know Bob Devaney well during his time as a regent.

Bob Devaney was quite possibly the most influential figure in the history of Nebraska football. Over the twenty years prior to Bob's arrival at the University of Nebraska in 1962, the football record was particularly dismal, with only one bowl appearance and that bowl appearance was due to the fact that Oklahoma, the league champion, was not allowed to go to a bowl game on two consecutive years. Since Oklahoma had won the previous year, Nebraska went to the Orange Bowl in 1954 and was beaten soundly by Duke. That 1965 football season would appear to be the bright spot of that twenty-year period. There were very few winning seasons and no outright championships. The year before Bob Devaney arrived, 1961, the University of Colorado came to Lincoln and held the University of Nebraska football team to no first downs and less than fifty yards of total offense as part of a season record of 361. In Bob's first season, 1962, Nebraska had a 92 record and went to the Gotham Bowl in New York City and beat the University of Miami on a very cold and windy day. Over his eleven-year coaching career at Nebraska, Bob Devaney won 82 percent of his games, eight conference championships and national championships in 1970 and 1971. Bob's hiring in 1962 started a forty-two-year stretch in which Nebraska was able to win many more games than any other school in Division I football and had a winning percentage of 82 percent, as opposed to Ohio State's second highest winning percentage of 75 percent.

Dick developed a very strong and lasting friendship with Bob Devaney, both while he was the head football coach of the University of Nebraska from 1962 through 1972 and during his tenure as Athletic Director for a number of years after concluding his coaching career. Dick was one of a handful of people who were able to communicate with Bob in such a way that Bob would be willing to step back and take a look at a different point of view when confronted with an issue that was troubling him. Bob had a great sense of humor and also at times had a temper that would lead him to take a position that was probably not in his best long-term interest and Dick was especially adept at diffusing such situations.

As time went on, Dick became progressively more interested in the academic mission of the Athletic Department and in 1989 endowed a fund to promote a student-athlete recognition banquet, which has become a staple of the Athletic Department calendar each year since. Dick and his brother Dale cooperated in establishing the fund. Dale has since passed away but Dick has continued to fund the academic banquet and many other academic programs. The first athletic banquet was held in 1991 at a bank in Lincoln before a small audience. Over the years the number of athletes honored and the faculty, coaches, and general public attending has grown tremendously. From 1992 to 1997, the academic banquet was held at the East Campus Student Union on the agricultural campus in the eastern part of Lincoln. From 1998 to 2012, the banquet was held at the Devaney Center, our basketball arena, which allowed a much larger crowd to attend. This past spring, 2013, the banquet was held at a hotel in downtown Lincoln. At that banquet, 259 student-athletes were honored. Every student-athlete who had better than a 3.0 grade point average was given a medallion to commemorate his or her academic achievement. Three levels of academic achievement were recognized. Those students with a 3.0–3.49 grade point average received a bronze medal, those achieving a 3.5–3.749 grade point average received a silver medal, and those with a 3.75–4.0 grade point average received a gold medal. There were eighty athletes who received the gold medal this last spring, indicating a very high level of academic achievement. It seems that any time an activity is recognized and valued, you get more of that activity and that has been the case with academic performance in the Athletic Department. We currently have a nation-leading 304 Academic All-Americans, which far surpasses any other NCAA school in the country, and much of that achievement is attributable to the recognition that Dick Herman and his family have provided.

In addition to having the largest number of Academic All-Americans, Nebraska leads the nation in the number of Top Eight Award winners with sixteen. The Top Eight Award is based upon academic and athletic excellence and community service. The Top Eight Award is similar in an academic context to the Heisman Trophy in football, as it is the highest award that the NCAA extends to a student–athlete.

The Hall of Distinction funded by Dick and his family has prominently recognized all aspects of academic achievement in our new Student Life Center. There are currently 5,648 University of Nebraska student-athletes who have graduated and lettered and all of these student-athletes are currently recognized in the Hall of Distinction, along with 116 postgraduate scholarship winners.

The Student Life Center was dedicated in October 2012 and is named the Dick and Peg Herman Family Student Life Complex in honor of all that Dick has done for Nebraska Athletics and our student-athletes. The Student Life Center contains state-of-the-art computer systems which are available to all of our student-athletes, as well as numerous study areas. Our student-athletes have access to UNL library materials and multiple software packages thanks to the technology available in the Student Life Center. This facility is nationally recognized by Athletic Management magazine as the national leader in academic centers and has enabled our student-athletes to attain a 3.167 overall grade point average this past year.

For the past several years, Dick has chartered an airplane and flown the football coaches' wives to one away game each year. He has been exceptionally kind and hospitable in providing transportation, not only through the airplane, but also in seeing to it that they have transportation from the airport to the stadium and back. I have witnessed several games with Dick in this context and have never once heard him say a critical word about coaches or players. He is truly a gentleman and is always positive and supportive regardless of the circumstance.

Dick has not only been generous to the academic program and the football program. He has been particularly supportive of all of our sports, including all thirteen women's sports provided by University of Nebraska Athletics. In 2011, Dick was given the Barbara Hibner Trailblazer Award, an award named after former Senior Women's Athletics Administrator Barbara Hibner, who for many years had overseen women's athletics in the Athletic Department.

Dick has always been a very strong family man and I was always impressed by Dick's devotion to his wife Peg as well as his children. Peg suffered a debilitating illness toward the end of her life and Dick would bring her to University of Nebraska football games in a wheelchair and was always very attentive and considerate of her needs. Peg developed a love of University of Nebraska Athletics over the course of time. As Dick shared his passion for Nebraska football with her, she eventually became a very strong fan. We appreciate all that Dick has done for University of Nebraska Athletics and in particular our academic programs. It is hard to adequately convey all that he has contributed in a few pages.

X.

Bridging the Centuries:
Looking Back . . . and Ahead

There is a great deal of debate these days about American exceptionalism—about who believes in it and who may have doubts. I have no doubts. But I also believe that the unique character of America is very much like my definition of patriotism. Love your country but always believe it can be improved.

—Tom Brokaw, *The Time of Our Lives*

People write memoirs for two reasons. The first is to recapture and relive the moments that shaped their lives; the second is to pass on to younger generations whatever lessons they've learned over the years.

In short, it's one part past, one part future, much like the feelings I experience whenever I visit the Nebraska campus at Lincoln. Physically it's far different from the place I knew as a student—much larger, with up to five times the student population. But the old landmarks remain, along with memories of the teachers and friends who touched my life those many years past.

I am in my tenth decade now. My life has bridged two centuries. But whatever your age, it's hard, if not impossible, to visit a college campus—especially one where you spent your own youth—without thinking not only of days gone by but the days ahead.

So it is that when I visit with and talk to today's young Americans—not just college students but young men and women in every walk of life—I wonder what lies ahead for them and for our country as the land of freedom and opportunity I knew as a youth.

I wonder, and I worry. Having seen our country survive the threats to our democratic way of life in the century past, I haven't any doubt about our ability to overcome whatever external threats face us now. It's the threat from within that concerns me—not domestic terrorism, but what I see as the slow and steady erosion of the political and family values that for over two centuries have made America, in Lincoln's words, "the last best hope of earth."

The focus of my concern lies in three areas, each affecting those values and institutions in its own destructive way.

(1) IKE'S WARNING AND "PERMANENT WAR"

Excerpt, address by President Dwight Eisenhower before the American Society of Newspaper Editors, April 1953:

Every gun that is made, every warship launched, every rocket fired signifies, in the final sense, a theft from those who hunger and are not fed, those who are cold and are not clothed.

This world in arms is not spending money alone. It is spending the sweat of its laborers, the genius of its scientists, the hopes of its children. The cost of one modern heavy bomber is this: a modern brick school in more than 30 cities. It is two electric power plants, each serving a town of 60,000 population. It is two fine, fully equipped hospitals.

It is some fifty miles of concrete pavement. We pay for a single fighter plane with a half-million bushels of wheat. We pay for a single destroyer with new homes that could have housed more than 8,000 people.

Those were President Dwight Eisenhower's words only three months after he took office. Eight years later, in his Farewell Address to the nation as our 34th president, Ike returned to that message by warning:

> In the councils of government, we must guard against the acquisition of unwarranted influence, whether sought or unsought, by the military-industrial complex. The potential for the disastrous rise of misplaced power exists and will persist.

Eisenhower was a prophet, but even he didn't foresee the breakup of the Soviet empire three decades later, leaving the United States as the world's only superpower. Moving into the 1990s, President George H. W. Bush could speak of a "peace dividend"—the freeing of hundreds of billions from the Pentagon budget to be put into the schools, hospitals, and highways Ike spoke of in 1953.

Unfortunately, that was not to be. More than two decades after the end of the Cold War, as military historian Andrew J. Bacevich points out, the United States still "spends as much or more money on its military than the entire rest of the world combined."

In his 2010 book, *Washington Rules: America's Path to Permanent War,* Bacevich, a retired Army colonel, points out that the United States also has approximately 300,000 troops stationed overseas, occupying or using over seven hundred military sites in thirty-nine countries—not including those in Iraq and Afghanistan.

Why should this be? The foreign threat facing our country today doesn't come in the form of a massive military force held by a hostile nation. The fight against terrorism—preventing another 9/11 and attacks against American interests overseas—can't be won by and doesn't require spending nearly $700 billion annually in conventional weapons and the upkeep of a global war machine.

What we're witnessing is Ike's warning—his prophecy—fulfilled. But make no mistake, it isn't just the Pentagon and its industrial partners pushing us down what Bacevich calls the "path to permanent war." In some cases it's our civilian rather than our military leaders providing the push.

Example: As Chairman of the Joint Chiefs of Staff in the Clinton administration, General Colin Powell resisted the idea of American military involvement in the Balkans. He saw it as a potential quagmire but was overruled by Secretary of State Madeleine Albright, who asked, "What's the point of having this superb military if we can't use it?"

Albright was so proud of that line that she even included it in her memoirs, insensitive to the fact that the "superb military" she wanted to use consists of young Americans who fight, bleed, are disabled, and die on foreign battlefields when sent into combat by leaders far removed from the battle zones.

Understand, as a Goldwater conservative who served in Eisenhower's army during World War II, I'm not one to ignore the need to defend our country's vital interests by military force. The problem, as Bacevich points out, is that we have a foreign policy based on the idea of American power being used not simply to defend our vital interests but to police the world.

And more: Not only police the world but, whether under a Republican Bush-Cheney administration or a Democratic Obama White House, spend tens of billions toward nation-building in the Middle East and across the globe—billions for schools, hospitals, and roads not in our own country, as Eisenhower wanted, but in countries like Iraq and Afghanistan (where, more often than not, money meant for construction goes into the pockets of corrupt officials and contractors).[1]

This isn't to argue that as the world's most powerful democracy, the "last best hope of earth," the United States has no responsibility or humanitarian interest beyond our borders. Nineteenth century isolationism in a 21st century world is not an option. But what those quick-on-the-trigger leaders in Washington—whether Democrats like Madeleine Albright or Republicans like Senator John McCain—should understand is that internationalism doesn't necessarily mean interventionism.

What can be done, after all these years, to take our country off the path to permanent war? Colonel Bacevich, one of the rare critics of the system who's actually seen how it works from inside the military, makes three proposals:

First, he says, our leaders need to understand that "the purpose of the

U.S. military is not to combat evil or remake the world but to defend the United States and its most vital interests"; *second*, our political leaders should stop using the U.S. military as a worldwide police force on the order of British imperial armies in the 19th century; *third*, the Pentagon's global footprint should shrink by employing force only as a last resort and only in self-defense—meaning we should never again follow the Bush-Cheney Doctrine of preventive war (as many of the voices that led us into Iraq now want to do in dealing with Iran).

I agree with all these proposals, but add a fourth: We should take steps to ensure that the burden of sacrifice and commitment to defend our country is shared by *all* Americans, not just a limited few.

★   ★   ★

Excerpt, headline and story from *The Washington Post*, March 2, 2011

LT. GEN. JOHN KELLY, WHO LOST SON TO WAR, SAYS U.S. LARGELY UNAWARE OF SACRIFICE
by Greg Jaffe

. . . Without once referring to his son's death, the general delivered a passionate and at times angry speech about the military's sacrifices and its troops' growing sense of isolation from society.

. . . Kelly is the most senior U.S. military officer to lose a son or daughter in Iraq or Afghanistan. He was giving voice to a growing concern among soldiers and Marines: The American public is largely unaware of the price its military pays to fight the United States' distant conflicts. Less than 1 percent of the population serves in uniform at a time when the country is engaged in one of the longest periods of sustained combat in its history.

I was against antiwar demonstrators in the 1960s and '70s, but now think they served a useful purpose. They reminded us that though we weren't being asked to make sacrifices here at home, there was a war going on overseas, with young Americans fighting and dying in Vietnam.

At the time this is written, the fighting in Afghanistan is now well into its second decade. But because less than 1 percent of the population is in uniform—and we aren't being taxed to pay for the war, it's still business-and-pleasure-as-usual on the American home front. Not to mention politics-as-usual in Washington.

Thanks to the fiscal irresponsibility of the Bush-Cheney administration, the Iraq-Afghanistan war is the first in history America has fought on a credit card; that's to say, we're taxing future generations to pay for it. Where, I ask, are the Republicans of today, who call themselves fiscal conservatives, on that issue? Nowhere to be heard. They raise their voices, loud and clear, against spending here at home—even against the food stamp program for the poor[2]—but the Pentagon budget, despite all evidence of waste and extravagance over the years, is seldom questioned.

There's a double standard at work here, one used by both parties. The Obama White House and Democrats in Congress are equally guilty of paving the path to permanent war, following policies that keep their voting constituencies insulated from the sacrifice made by those in uniform and their families.

SUPPORT OUR TROOPS read the bumper stickers. The people who put them on their cars and trucks, like home-front Americans in every war we've fought, are sincere in their hopes and prayers for our men and women in uniform. The difference today, as General Kelly points out, is in the level of support we give them:

- *In Afghanistan*, our National Guardsmen and reservists were called back for multiple tours of front-line duty because our military resources have been stretched to the limit and beyond by overseas commitments.

- *Here at home*, the level of support and care our leaders in Washington provide our disabled, homeless, and unemployed veterans is a national disgrace. Our leaders in Washington spare no expense in subsidizing wars but neglect the needs of those sent to fight them.

That said, how can we truly support our troops? Clearly, the status quo—words without action—won't do. Empty political rhetoric and bumper sticker slogans aside, it's time, I think, to go back to the future . . .

From the final report of President Nixon's Commission on an All-Volunteer Armed Force (1970):

(To) provide for the possibility of an emergency requiring a major increase in forces over an extended period, we recommend that machinery be created for a standby draft, to take effect by act of Congress upon the recommendation of the President.

The All-Volunteer Commission of 1970 was headed by Thomas Gates, Eisenhower's last Secretary of Defense (1959–1961). Like Ike, Gates and his fellow commissioners were clairvoyant: When reservists are being sent into Middle East combat zones for four to five tours of duty—as we've witnessed in recent years—I'd say we've arrived at that "emergency requiring a major increase in forces" foreseen by the Gates Commission.

In short, we need, as the Commission recommended, a standby draft to meet such emergencies.

It's no surprise that a former field commander like Lt. General Stanley McChrystal should agree with the Gates Commission's recommendation. But I have a grandson, David Jensen—twenty-four years old and eligible for such a call-up—who also thinks that restoring the draft is a good idea. In a personal essay he writes, "Knowing that all citizens will be affected by the decision to go to war, the nation will be less likely to enter into a war. The decision to go to war will be scrutinized and questioned by the public because of concern for family and friends."

Exactly. And I say this not just as a grandfather but as one of the remaining veterans of the last conflict our nation fought in which "the decision to go to war" was "scrutinized and questioned" in the way the Founding Fathers intended—not by executive decree or a mere congressional "resolution," but by a declaration under Article I, Section 8 of the Constitution.

Short of that, if our leaders in Washington mean to keep our nation on a permanent path to war, let the Obama White House and Congress do the next best thing: Follow the Gates Commission recommendation and *restore the draft.*

★   ★   ★

(2) CITIZENS UNITED AND ITS "CORRUPTING POTENTIAL"

Money is the mother's milk of politics.

—California political boss Jesse Unruh

If Jesse Unruh were around today he'd have to update his quote about money in politics. Thanks to the U.S. Supreme Court's 2010 ruling in *Citizens United v. Federal Elections Commission*, money today isn't the mother's milk but the corporate steroid of American politics.

By ruling 5 to 4 that corporate contributions to political campaigns are legally protected by the First Amendment, the Court, as Justice John Paul Stevens wrote in his dissenting opinion, rejected "the common sense of the American people, who have recognized a need to prevent corporations from undermining self-government since the founding, and who have fought against the distinctive corrupting potential of corporate electioneering since the days of Theodore Roosevelt."

Not that those in the private sector don't have the right to make their voices heard through political contributions. Having headed the National Beer Wholesalers PAC in the 1980s, I'd be the last to argue that. But the Court's ruling in *Citizens United* goes too far. It opens the floodgates to the "corrupting influence of corporate electioneering."

It's one thing to say that business interests have the First Amendment right to be heard in political campaigns; it's another to rule that any sector, public or private, has the right to drown out other voices and corrupt the process with unlimited campaign contributions . . .

*   *   *

2012 ELECTION SPENDING WILL REACH $6 BILLION

—Headline, October 31, 2012

The story beneath the headline quotes the executive director of the Center for Responsive Politics: "In the new campaign finance landscape post–Citizens United," she said, "we're seeing historic spending levels spurred by outside groups dominated by a small number of individuals and organizations making exceptional contributions."

Outside groups dominated by a small number of individuals: Experience tells me that such "exceptional contributions" guarantee undue influence on the candidate and, if elected, the office-holder who received them. What's more, by ruling that independent contributors can spend as much as they want, so long as their Super PACs aren't *directly connected* to a candidate or party, the Court effectively removed any restraining hand that responsible campaign officials might place in campaign ads run by outside groups.

In other words, political campaigns are guaranteed to become even dirtier and more negative in future years than they've been in the past.

That's what comes from having nine people on a Court who've had no working experience outside a courtroom, a law office, or a university classroom. Whatever their intention, a decision based on abstract theory rather than real political experience can end up doing more harm than good.

Wrong as it was, however, the Court's decision in *Citizens United* simply made a bad situation worse. Watching from the sidelines, I've seen what Justice Stevens called the "corrupting influence" of big money in politics grow at every level of government: When a candidate for the U.S. Senate in a small state like Maryland needs ten to fifteen million dollars just to be taken seriously, something's gone haywire. When it takes upward of thirty million dollars to run for the Senate in a state like Kentucky, our system is in trouble.

On that point, a word here about my experience in judging campaign contributions: The general rule is that when the average citizen contributes, anywhere from ten to a hundred dollars, he or she expects nothing in return but good government. But when multibillionaire businessmen spread hundreds of millions across the political board in an election year, they're looking for something more.

What saddens me most about this situation is that years ago I thought I'd done something to curb the "corrupting influence" of big money in politics.

In the early 1970s then Republican National Committee Chairman George H. W. Bush appointed me head of an RNC effort to work out a bipartisan solution to the problem of financing national party conventions. Traditionally, both Republican and Democratic conventions had been underwritten by corporate contributions. Together with my Democratic friends Bob Strauss and George Bristol, I headed for Capitol Hill to recommend a better way.

The year was 1974. Congress was considering legislation to provide for public financing of presidential elections through a payroll check-off system. Our job was to get national conventions included as part of the presidential election process.

It was by no means an easy sell. The idea of a payroll check-off in itself repelled many Republicans. Bob and George canvassed Democratic members in the House while I worked with Pennsylvania's Hugh Scott, the Republican Leader on the Senate side. Thanks to Scott, enough Republican votes swung our way to get the cost of conventions included in the final bill.

Bob, George, and I celebrated, thinking that with the passage of a public financing bill for presidential elections a bright new day was dawning in American politics. How little we knew.

★   ★   ★

OBAMA, ROMNEY AND THEIR PARTIES ON TRACK TO RAISE $2 BILLION

—Headline, The New York Times, *October 5, 2012*

In the same way we've entered into an era of permanent war it seems we're also caught up in what Brookings Institution scholars Norman Ornstein and Thomas Mann call "the permanent campaign."

Within days after Barack Obama was inaugurated for his second term as President, media speculation had already begun on who would run to succeed him in 2016. What's more, U.S. Senate and House members just sworn in for new terms were already busy raising money for the next election, two, four, or six years down the road.

Campaigning, it seems, never stops. But for those too young to know otherwise, there was a time when presidential candidate debates and big-dollar advertising didn't show up on TV a year and a half before Election Day.

All this costs money. Big money. Enough so that the need to raise ever-larger amounts led both major presidential candidates in 2012 to turn down public in favor of private funding. Obama had done the same running against John McCain in 2008. Four years later, after being re-elected, he became the first president to form his own Super PAC, called Priorities USA Action.

Meanwhile, working the other side of the fund-raising street, Karl Rove's American Crossroads, an anti-Obama Super PAC, raised $106

million during the 2012 election cycle—under the loosely written pro-
visions of Section 501(c) (4) of the Internal Revenue tax code. All legal,
but carrying with it what Justice Stevens called "the distinctive corrupting potential of corporate electioneering."

Can anything be done about it? Yes, it can—but only if "the common
sense of the American people" takes hold. We can (1) get a Supreme
Court majority that will reverse *Citizens United*, and, until that comes
about, (2) amend Section 501(c)(4) of the tax code so that the identities
of anonymous big money contributors to political campaigns become
known to the public.

To my mind, that's only common sense: If big corporate contributions are given the right to have their voices heard under the First
Amendment, it follows that voters have the right to know whose voice
it is they're listening to.

★   ★   ★

(3) PARTISAN POLITICS AND THE PERMANENT CAMPAIGN

The single most important thing we want to achieve is
for President Obama to be a one-term President.

—Senate Republican leader Mitch McConnell, October 25, 2010

Gridlock. No compromise. Constant bickering and stalemate, not
only between Capitol Hill and the White House but between the two
branches of Congress. The only thing that everybody in Washington can
agree on these days is that Washington is broken.

Again, for those too young to remember otherwise, it wasn't always
this way. There were drawn-out battles between the White House and
Congress, yes, legislative fights on Capitol Hill that brought on heated
debates, and even, from time to time, filibusters and showdowns.

But things got done. Bills were passed. Budgets were approved by the

House. Presidential nominees were given an up-or-down vote by the full Senate. And at the end of each legislative day, no matter how heated the debate that had taken place, Republican and Democratic leaders would get together—in the case of Everett Dirksen and Lyndon Johnson in the 1950s, over Scotch-and-water in Johnson's office—to discuss their differences and work out a compromise.

Three decades later, that bipartisan tradition continued—though minus the whiskey—when Republican Bob Dole and Democrat George Mitchell worked together to get things done in the Senate during the Reagan-Bush years. Collegiality, not personal hostility, was the rule.

Example: As everyone familiar with the Senate knows, office size is all-important to its ego-driven members. But when the Democrats took over the Senate in 1989 and Mitchell replaced Dole as Majority Leader, the usual transfer of offices—Dole moving out and Mitchell moving into to the spacious Majority Leader's office—didn't take place. As Dole told me at a nonpolitical event attended by both men, when time came for the move Mitchell told him it wouldn't be necessary—Bob could stay in the larger office while George operated as Majority Leader out of a smaller office.

Can anybody see that happening today between Mitch McConnell and Harry Reid? Or, another example, House Speaker John Boehner visiting with President Obama, as Democratic Speaker Tip O'Neill did with President Reagan in the 1980s, to break a legislative logjam? No chance, because even when Boehner and Obama do get together, whether at the White House or on a golf course, nothing can come of it. Boehner, as we've seen time and again, is a party leader in name only. He heads a Republican House caucus composed in large part of members who call themselves conservatives but make a mockery of the institutions and principles that true conservatives value.

True conservatives work to limit the power of government, not shut it down if they don't get their way. True conservatives don't paralyze the American political process by closing their minds to any other point of view, even within their own party.

When Chuck Hagel, a former Republican Senator and a Vietnam War hero, came up for confirmation as Secretary of Defense in early 2013, he was subject to a bitter, at times personal, attack before being confirmed—an attack led not by Democrats who didn't want to see a Republican appointed to the job, but by Republicans opposed to anyone having anything to do with the Obama administration.

The same was true when New Jersey Governor Chris Christie publicly appeared with President Obama to thank him for rushing federal aid to his state following Hurricane Sandy in the fall of 2012.

As a Goldwater conservative I've always shared Barry's view that whatever your political differences with others, "You can disagree without being disagreeable." Though poles apart from John F. Kennedy in political philosophy, he and Kennedy were personal friends. Where the larger interests of the country were concerned Barry had no problem working with Democrats, as he did with Georgia Senator San Nunn on national defense issues.

Those in Washington today who consider "compromise" a dirty political word—to the extent that they'd see our country default on the national debt rather reach an agreement on fiscal issues—aren't to my mind conservatives, but a mirror image of the left-wing radicals who almost brought the Democratic Party to ruins in the 1960s. They need to restudy the history of the Constitutional Convention of 1789. The Founding Fathers, they'll discover, were principled but practical men who framed our Constitution after fierce debate followed by compromise.

Our-way-or-no-way is the political philosophy of totalitarianism states, not free societies.

★   ★   ★

Working across party lines for the common good is often just a matter of thinking outside the box. That was the case when I worked with Bob Strauss and George Bristol on campaign finance reform and on other occasions during my active political days when I saw an opportunity to get things done in the national interest.

One occasion that comes to mind involved my working with South Dakota Senator Tom Daschle, then Democratic Majority Leader, on the minimum wage issue. Peg and I had acquired a place in Dakota Dunes, South Dakota, and I'd come to know Tom on a personal as well as political basis. Though viewed as an ultraliberal in some Republican circles, Tom was a moderate on key issues, a heartlander who didn't let ideology blind him as Majority Leader.

My position on the minimum wage issue put me, as a conservative and a businessman, on the maverick side of both my political and business friends. Having come up the hard way, I was sympathetic to the need for a living wage for working families. On learning Tom was only four or five votes short of approval for a minimum wage increase, I came up with an out-of-the-box idea to put the bill over: Tie the increase to a reduction of the capital gains tax, something Republicans in the Senate could go for as an everybody-wins trade-off.

Tom thought it was a great idea, as did the Clinton White House. But this was the age of gridlock, and members of my own party in the Senate wouldn't hear of it. There would be no compromise on any issue—even one that included a tax break that Republicans favored—if it meant that Democrats might gain some benefit.

Not to lay the blame for Washington gridlock at the feet of one party alone. Senate Democrats under the leadership of Nevada's Harry Reid play the same game when it suits their partisan interests. The difference is that members of the no-compromise faction of today's GOP carry their philosophy into intraparty disputes. When good conservatives like Bob Bennett of Utah and Dick Lugar of Indiana lose their Senate seats in primaries because they don't march in ideological lockstep with the Tea Party, something has seriously gone wrong with the Republican Party I knew from the 1950s through the 1990s.

Conceded, there were some conservatives in those days who took a hard-line view of the role played by Eastern liberals in the party. But I wasn't one of them: Elsie Hillman, a stalwart in the Pennsylvania party, and I have been friends and coworkers in too many campaigns to remember, while Bill Scranton and I came to know and respect each other, despite our differences, at the '64 convention. A chance meeting with Nelson Rockefeller at the '76 convention in Kansas City—we shared our views in a waiting room over cold coffee in styrofoam cups—led to a similar understanding.

All this fit a personal pattern. Throughout my life, whether in politics or business, I've always felt that the best way to get things done is by finding common ground with those who hold different views; at the very least, as Barry Goldwater said, to be able to disagree without being disagreeable.

★   ★   ★

Getting it done. Finding a way to make things work. If asked the key to whatever success I've had in life, that would be my answer. Whether on a troop ship headed for North Africa, at a bargaining table with the president of the Teamsters, or in a backstage room in a convention center, I've worked at being a problem-solver.

That said, what would my answer be if asked to solve the problem of gridlock in Washington? How can we get things working again in our Nation's Capital?

First, I'd say, we need to step back and recognize the source of the problem—the permanent campaign. It's foolish to talk about bipartisan cooperation if those we send to Washington, like Mitch McConnell, are focused solely on the next election. Campaigns are about getting and holding onto power. The longer they go on, the more bitter and divisive they become.

The question then is what needs to be done to end the cycle of nonstop campaigning? And the answer to that, even for a longtime problem-solver, doesn't come easy. A multibillion dollar industry has grown out of the permanent campaign, with a special-interest army of highly paid consultants, pollsters, and ad agencies eager to keep the dollars flowing.

Which leads us back to the problem posed by money—big money—in today's politics, and the need for campaign finance reform: Limit the flow of money into campaign coffers and you limit the time needed both to raise and spend it. Even Mitch McConnell would have to concede that.

Not to say that the sole answer to solving the problem of gridlock in Washington lies in reversing the decision in *Citizens United* and curbing campaign contributions. That would be a starter. But in the oldest, greatest constitutional democracy on earth there's only one true problem-solver when it comes shaking things up in Washington—the voice of the American people.

★   ★   ★

History tells us that as Benjamin Franklin was leaving the hall after the final session of the Constitutional Convention he was approached by a woman who asked whether the delegates had voted in favor of a monarchy or a republic.

"A republic," was Franklin's answer, "if you can keep it."

At age eighty-one, Franklin was the oldest of the Founding Fathers and had lived long enough to be a realist. He had seen his country win its freedom, but the challenge, he knew, would be to keep it.

And more: "The Constitution," he would say, "doesn't guarantee happiness, only the pursuit of it. You have to catch up with it yourself."

Plain words, but a perfect expression of the heartland philosophy taught me as a young boy growing up in Fremont, Nebraska, two centuries later. There are no guarantees, I was told by my elders, just opportunities.

The pursuit of happiness and the opportunity to "catch up with it yourself" are what set our country apart from all the other nations. It's the American journey promised by our Constitution to every young

American—a journey I've taken and worked to see my grandchildren and future generations of Americans take.

And take it they will, of that I'm sure. I recall as a young man of sixteen hearing President Roosevelt say that my generation had "a rendezvous with destiny." Looking back, the same could be said of every generation of Americans from Ben Franklin's day to the present. Blessed with freedom, we're challenged to pass the blessing on, through the worst and best of times, whatever it takes.

My generation, it was said by Tom Brokaw, was America's greatest. Perhaps so, but as an American heartlander I remain an optimist: Even greater generations lie ahead.

★ ★ ★

Acknowledgments

Special thanks to **Jim Baker** and **Tom Osborne** for their contributions to this memoir. No memoir covering over half a century can be complete without the help of those whose shared experience has enriched one's life. With that in mind, heartfelt thanks also go to:

Randy Ferlic, my closest friend and verbal jousting partner, who recalled our heated, though civil, late-night debates sorting out our differences over politics and the social order while our wives, Peg and Terry, provided a patient audience. One of the country's finest surgeons, it was Randy who eloquently delivered the eulogy at Peg's funeral, words that have stayed with me through the years.

Stu Spencer, the legendary political consultant in the field of modern campaign management. My good friend and old adversary from the Goldwater-Rockefeller battle for delegates in 1964, Stu provided his expert insight into not only that campaign but others from years gone by.

Dan Sullivan, my invaluable assistant at the 1972 convention, who went on to a successful career in Washington as a presidential aide and whose recollection of the Nixon, Ford, and Bush 41 years helped refresh my own recollection of that period.

Leon Parma and **Miles Harvey** gave generously of their time in recalling the events and incidents that led to my decision to move the 1972 convention from San Diego to Miami.

Thanks also to **Rita E. Siemers** for her tireless efforts in providing transcripts and editorial assistance throughout the preparation of the book.

Finally, no acknowledgment would be complete without mention of those closest who provided support and encouragement along the journey's way. Words alone cannot express my appreciation and affection for **Leonardo** and **Ninfa Policarpio**, a caring couple who came into the Herman family orbit in Peg's late years.

And, of course, there is the family itself—Peg's sister **Nan**, whose counsel I value and friendship I cherish, along with my loving children, **Catherine**, **Anne**, **Rick,** and **Mike**, our eight grandchildren and seven great-grandchildren. May their years ahead be bright and blessed in this new American century.

—Dick Herman
October, 2013

Notes

CHAPTER III
1. Rick Atkinson, *An Army at Dawn*.

CHAPTER IV
1. How extensive was the rail industry's effort? It took in not only competition from truck operators on the nation's highways but waterway transportation as well. Along with fighting against construction of the federal highway system, the railroads resisted another favored Eisenhower Administration project, completion of the St. Lawrence Seaway.

CHAPTER V
1. Paul was not only a master strategist in state politics but his influence was felt in national politics as well in working out the federal-state tax formula applied to the Eisenhower Interstate Highway System.
2. Small world department: Charlie, it turned out, was on the same troop ship to North Africa I was on in November 1942. Probably one of the hungry GIs I helped shepherd to the ship's mess hall.

CHAPTER VI
1. About Hubert Humphrey: Whatever differences I had with him politically, I always felt he was one of the most admirable national leaders of his time. The way I put it to friends, my idea of self-improvement would be to have Dick Nixon's brain and Hubert Humphrey's heart.

CHAPTER VII
1. It was well-known in Washington at the time that John was constantly distracted by the erratic behavior of his wife, Martha.

CHAPTER VIII
1. To Ford backers, Sears' proposal was known as the "misery loves company" amendment. It had been the Reagan strategist's brainstorm earlier in the campaign to announce that Pennsylvania Senator Richard Schweiker would be Reagan's running

mate. The choice of Schweiker, a Pennsylvania liberal, had angered many conservatives and Sears no doubt hoped any choice Ford made would do the same.

2. One of Washington's top political get-togethers, held each year.

CHAPTER X

1. According to *The New York Times* (July 5, 2013), despite the Karzai government's known corruption the Obama administration asked for "$3.4 billion more for Afghanistan in 2014" which "would put the pot for reconstruction available in that country at $20 billion." That's $20 billion going into a Middle East sinkhole while a federal "sequester" at the same time is cutting funds for rebuilding schools, hospitals, and the infrastructure in our own country.

2. A food stamp program, let's not forget, that came out of the bipartisan efforts of Senators Bob Dole of Kansas and George McGovern of South Dakota.